FUN(D)RAISING

150 Money Making Ideas

STACEY RITZ

Fundraising for Non-Profits: 150 Money Making Ideas
Stacey Ritz.
Published by Rockville Publishing

Front cover photo credit istockphotos
Back cover photo credits istockphotos, A4A Inc.

ISBN: 978-1511453127

PRINTED IN THE UNITED STATES OF AMERICA

ROCKVILLE
PUBLISHING

Dedicated to Mom and Dad
For teaching me the value of hard work

"If you want to build a ship, don't drum up the men to gather wood, divide the work and give orders. Instead, teach them to yearn for the vast and endless sea."

-Antoine de Saint-Exupery

TABLE OF CONTENTS

FORWARD

Lifelong learners are lifelong earners. As the co-founder and Executive Director of a 501(c)3 non-profit organization, it has been vital that we find enjoyable and sustainable fundraisers to support our viable programs. Every year we continue to read, learn and experiment with new fundraising ideas for our organization. A fundraising event that works for one organization may not work for another. The fact is: some ideas work, some don't. When we find a fundraiser that works for us, we stick with it. But we're always on the hunt for innovative, new ideas that we can add and incorporate into our schedule.

Most likely you've picked up this book because you're in search of new ideas. Whether you are a start-up non-profit (i.e. for-purpose) organization, a seasoned organization/cause or an individual seeking fundraising ideas, introducing new fundraisers to your organization can only serve to attract additional donors. And who couldn't use more donors?

Fundraising events not only raise funds for your organization, but they also help grow your donor base. Hosting a fundraiser event - whether online or in person – draws people to your organization. Events, done correctly, pique curiosity; and curiosity can translate into new donors.

Fun(d)raising: 150 Money Making Ideas shares specific fundraising ideas and events that are effective for any non-profit organization, school or cause.

Whether you volunteer with a children's charity or an animal rescue, the ideas brought forth will enhance your organizations earnings. With creative ideas and helpful insight, you will find everything from tips on coordinating fundraisers to ways to attract potential donors to your events. If you're in search of fundraising ideas for your organization - keep reading. Everything you need to know is right at your fingertips - including a boost of motivation!

NOTE: While you are welcome to read this book straight through, you may prefer to flip through the pages to the fundraisers that most interest you now. This is a reference book that you can refer to time and again as you plan future fundraisers and continue the work that you're doing in the community.

COORDINATING FUNDRAISERS

Every organization needs a leader and every fundraising event needs a coordinator. Leadership is essential with each event. Being organized and informed are key to your event's success, as well.

Put yourself in the shoes of a potential donor. Imagine that you show up for a 5K Run/Walk to benefit a local charity. You initially found the charity on social media, but you're interested in learning more about what they do in your community. When you show up to the 5K event, if you find the registration table empty and the environment in total disarray, your impression of the organization is impacted in a negative way. When you finally track down a volunteer and ask about what the organization does in the community, if you are given a confusing or a blunt unenthusiastic reply, you will most likely form an unfavorable opinion of the organization. On the other hand, if you arrive at the 5K event and you're greeted with a friendly hello, if the registration table is full of cheerful volunteers ready to assist participants, you will instantly feel a part of something magical.

We are emotional creatures. Perhaps Maya Angelou said it best, "I've learned that people will forget what you said, people will forget what you did, but people will never forget how you made them feel." While it's important for event volunteers to know what the organization stands for and to adequately communicate that to potential donors, it's equally as vital for volunteers to be excited about the organization's program(s). Energy is contagious. When your event coordinator exudes a positive and cheerful attitude, volunteers will too. And excited volunteers lead to excited donors.

Having an upbeat and organized event coordinator is essential to hosting a successful event. The event coordinator should have strong communication skills, along with ample energy and a strong focus on the fundraiser itself.

Remember, hosting a fundraiser event for your school, cause or organization is a fun experience!

Here are a few key points for event coordinators to remember:

- Stay organized
- Know who your volunteers are and how they can best assist with the event. What are their talents? What do they enjoy?
- If your fundraising event allows for pre-registration, be sure to keep an accurate list (and a back-up) of those who have pre-registered.
- How will you boost morale for this particular event? (i.e. Is it in the budget to purchase t-shirts for event volunteers?)
- How will you increase ticket sales for the event? Create a plan and actively communicate the plan to event volunteers. This is a group effort!

- Take time to write your vision for the big day. How will attendees be greeted? Where will they check-in? What is the itinerary? Do you have plenty of volunteers committed to coming to the event? Do you have additional volunteers in case an unforeseen need arises? (*They almost always occur!*)
- How will you signal the end of the event?
- Imagine yourself as an attendee of this event: what would you like to experience? How would you like to feel? Take these thoughts into consideration during event planning.
- Follow through. If you say you will arrive at 7AM, arrive at 6:45AM. Consistently doing what you say builds credibility and trust with your volunteers and donors, creating a winning situation for the organization.
- Stay calm. Yes, it is easier said than done! Planning for an event takes dedication and time. But no matter how much time you pour into your planning and preparation, undoubtedly, something will go wrong on event day. Take a deep breath; it's okay! As the event coordinator, it is important to remain calm under pressure. Volunteers will come to you with minor crises on event day and perhaps larger crises that arise, but as entrepreneur and host of Marie TV, Marie Forleo has said, "everything is figureoutable." If you've organized and prepared for the event, you can tackle any issue that arises. Did you run out of blue ribbons to add to your event programs? Maybe you forgot your box

of volunteer t-shirts. It will all be okay. Stay calm and keep focused on the goal; to raise money for a good cause and create a fun-filled experience for both volunteers and attendees.

- Thank everyone. Yes, everyone. Thank your volunteers. Thank every attendee. Thank donors. Thank those who ask about your organization. Although they may not donate today, they may become a life-long supporter tomorrow. Connection matters and when you extend sincere gratitude, great things will happen.

WEBSITE

Did you know that people form an opinion about your organization in the first three-seconds of viewing your website? Three-seconds! Your organization may not know how to write code, but there are many user-friendly Internet sites that make it simple to create a fresh, appealing site that can influence your potential supporters.

The front page of your organizations website should absolutely include the following:

- Organization's name
- Mission statement
- Contact information
- Location(s) served

Visual appeal is essential. Remember, you have three-seconds to win potential donors. While this book supplies you with 150 fundraising ideas for your school, cause or for-purpose organization, don't overlook the importance of your website. Don't assume that you must spend thousands of dollars to have a professional looking site. Today, we have countless programs that make creating a website incredibly affordable (in some cases, free!) and easy to learn.

As you plan your annual fundraising events, your website is a great place to let supporters know of upcoming gatherings. Create a webpage within your site for each fundraiser you host throughout the year.

Draw attention to that page during the quarter in which the event will take place. You can also create specific fundraising pages to correlate with your events on websites such as *GoFundMe* (www.gofundme.com) and *YouCaring* (www.youcaring.com).

SMALL TO MEDIUM FUNDRAISERS

SMALL TO MEDIUM FUNDRAISERS

Don't let the word "small" fool you! Small doesn't have to coordinate with miniscule funds being raised. Starting small is often the key to success in any endeavor. Utilize your volunteer's skill sets. Do you have a group of college students who want to participate in a fun outdoor fundraiser for your charity? Why not coordinate a car wash event? Car wash events can boast $1,000 or more in funds. In addition to proper coordination, it's all about location, location, location. Choose high traffic venues with easy access and adequate visibility.

Do you have a volunteer who is a professional photographer? Consider creating a photo event at your local park. While the event itself is fairly simple, if done correctly, you have the potential of raising $500 or more.

In this section, you will find fifty fun money-making ideas for your organization. The ideas can work for virtually any school, cause or non-profit organization. If an idea resonates with you, take some time to think about how you can tailor the event to fit into your organization's theme. For example, if you are an animal rescue charity and you want to focus awareness on your *BEAT THE HEAT: Spay and Neuter Early* campaign, work with a local business/corporation. Ask that they allow employees to wear shorts on a specific Friday, if an employee donates $5 to your charity. You can tie in your BEAT THE HEAT theme with the summer season and the perk of wearing shorts to work. It's an enjoyable and winning situation for everyone.

Regardless of your organizations size, the following money-making ideas can boost morale, create funds and draw attention to the important work your group performs in the community. Now, let's get started!

CAR WASH

A successful car wash event can yield up to $1,000 if held in the right location. What is the *right* location? Choose to hold your car wash at a business that has a lot of daily traffic and is near a main road. Donors attending car wash events will be spur-of-the-moment attendees. Having a highly visible, easily accessible location is crucial to your success.

Plan ahead! Do you have enough volunteers committed to washing cars? Do you have volunteers who are willing to hold up signs, inviting the public to come to your car wash fundraiser?

Prior the event, be sure you have gathered enough supplies. Do you have enough soap, rags, and sponges? Plan to bring more than you think you will need. If you have underage volunteers, be sure to have proper parental supervision.

Know the flow: have a clear entrance and exit for cars attending your fundraiser. If you plan on having a large crowd (and we hope you do!), consider establishing multiple entrance points and multiple vehicle washing stations. Speed and efficiencies are not to be underrated. Set up a drying area inviting cars to pull forward after being washed; you do not want the drying process to slow down your flow.

Items we recommend having at your event:

*Squeegees
*Donation Jar
*Money collector (with ample change available)
*Hoses (be sure they are long enough)
*1 or 2 lanes for car washing
*Designated area for drying
*Designated entrance and exist areas (to maintain a smooth flow)
*5 gallon buckets (several)
*Towels (ask each volunteer to bring 3-5)
*Soap
*Sponges (lamb's wool squares are recommended)
*Pre-made signs to have volunteers bring in cars (gather together to create the signs a night or two in advance)
*Signage to designate entrance area
*Signage to designate drying area
*Window cleaner

Signage should include words such as:

*Low Price
*Best
*Wow
*Look!
*Support
*Community
*Big
*Great Deal!

Assign a specific person(s) to handle the money. Have enough cash on hand to make change. Also, keep a large donation jar in an accessible location where attendees can donate additional funds (and to allow those walking by without a vehicle to donate to your cause, if they wish).

You can hold an adjoining bake sale during the car wash if you wish. Just be sure to have a separate group of volunteers to monitor the bake sale table and funds during the event. This can bring in additional funds as drivers may purchase baked goods while waiting for their car to be washed.

It should go without saying, but the event should be fun for everyone involved. Although you are there to do a job (wash cars and raise money for a good cause), the more fun your volunteers and attendees have, the better they will feel about the organization you are supporting. Remember, people remember how you make them feel.

It's a good idea to ask every volunteer to wear matching t-shirts. Whether it's the organizations shirt or a solid color (i.e. bright green); uniformity will make it easier for attendees to know who volunteers on behalf of the organization and it will make your event more visible to those driving by.

Don't forget to bring flyers or cards to hand out to everyone who attends your car wash. Flyers can say THANK YOU and request that attendees visit your website or social media page(s). You want to give attendees something to let them know what your organization does within your community.

Ideas for driving traffic to your event:

*Have volunteers hold signs near the road, directing people to have their car washed.
*Hang flyers at other local businesses on the day of your event.
*Submit a press release to your local newspaper prior to the event (ask that it be published on the day of your car wash).
*Post a flyer on your social media pages and on your website.
*Ask volunteers to spread the word to their friends, family and co-workers.

PHOTOS WITH SANTA

Photos with Santa or the Easter Bunny can be highly successful events that work for a wide variety of groups and charities. For example, animal welfare charities can encourage pets to attend for special photos. As with all event fundraisers, location is essential. Finding a high traffic area is imperative to hosting a successful, money-making event. Consider collaborating with a high traffic store to host your holiday photo event.

Find a great photographer:
Do you have a volunteer photographer (or two? It never hurts to have a back-up) who is interested in taking photos during your fundraiser? Have you previously viewed their work? Do they have equipment to print the photos instantly?

Finding a jolly Santa or Easter Bunny:
Do you have a volunteer for this role? You may want to locate a volunteer to dress up as a happy helper, too (i.e. elf). Happy helpers can come in handy, helping pets look toward the camera or helping children smile. Again, it never hurts to have a back-up. If your designated volunteer Santa becomes ill on your event day, you will need to have someone to fill the role. It's important for your volunteer to be cheerful and patient.

Props:
Have a variety of props on hand. If your event is pet friendly, have a wide variety of pet toys to entice pets to look toward the camera. It's always a good idea to have child-friendly toys on hand as well.

If children are hesitant to have their photo taken with Santa, invite them to watch several other children have their photos taken, before they climb onto Santa's lap. Have your Santa ask the child questions (i.e. What do they want for Christmas? Do they set cookies out for Santa on Christmas Eve?).

Saturdays in December are usually the best time to hold a *Photos with Santa* event. For Easter photos, the weekend before Easter tends to yield the best results. Generally, the 10 AM – 2 PM time range draws the largest crowd.

As with any event, you'll need to advertise. Utilize your e-mail list, social media, website and post flyers throughout your town one week prior to the event. Ask volunteers to invite their friends, family and co-workers. Going door-to-door to hand out flyers for the event in local neighborhoods can increase awareness as well.

GIFT WRAPPING

The holidays bring ample shopping. As the holiday rush increases, shoppers become anxious with their growing *to do* lists. When you offer a gift wrapping service to busy shoppers, it's a winning situation for everyone! When shoppers know their donation is going to a local charity, and you're helping them save time and energy by doing the wrapping for them, you'll drum up business quickly.

Find a busy local store and ask to partner with them. Will they allow you to set up a gift wrapping booth near the exit? Let them know your plan. What days will you have volunteers at the booth? How many volunteers will be working at one time? What kind of signage will you have? In less than three-minutes, let the store owner know the mission of your organization and how this specific fundraiser, in their store, will benefit the local community. Be sure to let the store owner know how the event will benefit *them* (i.e. posting a free ad for their business on your website, bringing in additional customers from your supporter base).

When gift wrapping, it is essential that you maintain a professional appearance. Below are a few suggestions:

*2 volunteers should operate the gift wrapping booth/table at all times.
*Volunteers should wear the same shirt (displaying your organization's name).

*Offer several different wrapping paper options. Prepare by having double the amount of wrapping paper you plan on using (it goes faster than you think)!

*Bring a lot of tape.

*Have a minimum of 2 scissors available for volunteers.

*Display a large professional banner for your organization at the front of the table.

*Display a large GIFT WRAPPING FOR... sign at your table to draw in business.

*Ask the store's check-out lanes to offer a flyer to every customer and direct them to your gift wrapping table.

*Have a large donation jar prominently displayed.

*Bring change.

*Allow gift wrapping attendees to donate via cash, check or credit card.

*Have ample business cards for your charity – for attendees to take with them.

RUMMAGE SALE

Get the word out! Advertise in your local paper, hang flyers at local businesses, post multiple times on your social media pages and create a banner for the front page of your website. Let the community know about your event and exactly how the proceeds will benefit lives in your area. On your flyers, be sure to clearly state the date, time, address and directions. List the types of items buyers can expect to find at your rummage sale. Also include the name of your organization on the flyers.

Rummage sales are a fun way to raise money for worthy causes. Plan ahead and collect donated items for your event several weeks (or months) in advance. It is best if you can have a team of volunteers who are willing and able to drive to donors homes to pick up the donated items. If you have a drop off location for items, this is also helpful.

Be sure your items are clean and presentable. Product organization (i.e. all books are fifty-cents) is helpful in gaining additional sales. Set out a large donation jar for attendees to leave an extra donation to your organization (even if they don't find a treasure to take home that day). Along with the donation jar, keep a knowledgeable volunteer nearby as well as plenty of flyers and marketing materials for your organization. Letting people know about your organization can turn rummage sale visitors into lifetime donors.

Another strategy that can yield higher proceeds at your event is to hold a BOGO sale at your rummage sale. If your rummage sale is a two-day event, announce on the second day that everything is B.O.G.O. (*Buy One, Get One* - buy a shirt, get a shirt).

As with all events, location is crucial to your success. Choose a high traffic area, preferably near a busy roadway. Choosing the right location has the potential to double or triple your sales.

PAINTING

Throw a paint party! You don't have to be Picasso to paint. It's not about creating a masterpiece; it's about having fun and raising funds and awareness for your charity. There are many ways to host a paint party for your organization. If you have a large, open space at your facility (or if you have access to a spacious area) you can host an event yourself. Purchase a canvas and several sizes of paint brushes (recommended 2-3) for each attendee. Rather than making a guess, require that attendee's pre-register for the event at least one week in advance; this way you will know how many supplies to have available. You will also want to have plenty of paper towels. Other recommended items for each participant: small easel, smock or apron. Of course you will need paint, too! Purchasing large tubes of paint is often more affordable than individual paint sets for participants. Use paper plates to provide the right amount of paint needed for each guest.

You'll need to have a volunteer who knows *how* to paint. Have that volunteer develop a basic painting that he/she can teach to attendees on the night of your event. Boost the mood by playing upbeat music during the event and offer a side table of drinks and baked goods as a bonus (you can even ask attendees to each bring an item for the table).

Set a ticket price, get the word out and start gathering attendees for a successful and fun event!

If you're interested in having a professional company host your event, try contacting businesses like *Pinot's Pallet*. The company specializes in hosting events and many work with local non-profit organizations to host fundraiser nights (where they donate a percentage of proceeds from every ticket sold, to your organization). The benefit of utilizing a professional company is that you only have to plan the event and bring people. The company will supply the tools and you can sit back and enjoy the evening!

LOCAL BUSINESS PARTNER

We spend much of our life online. While the Internet is an amazing place to network and raise funds, going outside and meeting the local businesses in your own back yard can yield positive results for your cause, school or charity, too.

Introducing yourself to businesses in your area is a great way to spread the word about your organization and meet potential partners. What is a local business partner? Collaborating with a local business is rewarding for your group. If you want to collect food donations for your charity, ask a local grocer if you can place a food barrel in their store. Or you may want to start even smaller and ask your local bookstore if they will set out your donation jar by their check-out register. There are a million creative ways to partner with local businesses to raise funds and awareness for your organization. Think outside of the box and create an idea that works for your group and then go and introduce yourself (always be sure to leave your card or flyer with each business). Collaborative efforts can only serve to benefit your mission of helping the local community.

CREATIVE YOUTUBE VIDEOS

You don't need professional equipment to create a video that will reach the world. But you do need creativity and effort! Can you create an upbeat video that draws positive attention to your organization? Can you create that video in under thirty-seconds? Using a catchy tune can help sustain your viewer's attention.

Are you musical or do you have a musically inclined volunteer? Reach out to your supporters and combine your talents. Most cell phones will record short videos today. Start simple. Create a thirty-second video about your organization. Test the waters and share your video on social media pages to begin spreading the word. At the end of the video direct people to your charity's website and ask them to consider donating. Let them know that even $5 is helpful.

Once you've launched your first video, try a second. The more videos you add, the more supporters you will attract. In time, consider purchasing a basic editing program, but it's certainly not necessary to produce a catchy video that can bring in funds for your cause. This is an entertaining and enjoyable fundraising activity that utilizes free online programs (i.e.YouTube, Facebook, Twitter). Creating a video for your organization can also help to boost morale within your organization, and bring volunteers together for a worthy cause.

NEWSLETTER/EMAIL LIST

If you don't have a regular newsletter publication for your cause, school or charity, it is highly recommended that you keep an ongoing e-mail list. Create a page on your website to invite supporters to sign up for your e-mail (and/or newsletter) list. When you first start collecting e-mail addresses, spread the word using social media. Ask potential supporters: *Do you want to have free parenting tips delivered straight to your inbox? Sign up today for our e-mail list. It's free!* (You can fill in the type of tips you will be supplying, based on the nature of your group).

Your list will grow organically overtime. It's important to remember not to abuse the list. Most of us do not want daily e-mails on a specific topic. Studies have proven consistency is important when sending group emails, but emails that come too frequently are often deleted. Whether you're sending e-mails to your list once a week or once a quarter, try to stay consistent so that your supporters know what they can expect from you. Also, keep the information in your e-mails concise, informative, interesting and relevant to your readers. Supporters sign up for your e-mail list because they want to know what your group is doing to help the community. Keep it focused and easy to read. If you wish to share longer stories, share a snippet of the story in your e-mail and add a *read more* link.

While newsletter and/or email lists are not always a direct source of donations, they help build trust and credibility for your organization. Supporters want to know that you are transparent and that their funds are truly being used for a good cause. Sharing inspiring stories of your work will allow your readers to understand the value that you bring to the community. Your emails and newsletters can also easily be forwarded and shared with others, helping spread the word about your great work. Don't forget to add a direct link for donations at the bottom of every e-mail/newsletter.

As a side note, always be sure to offer an unsubscribe option at the bottom of your e-mails/newsletter (for those who wish to no longer receive your e-mails). Be sure those receiving your emails have an interest in your cause. Put yourself in the reader's shoes, be respectful and courteous and keep doing great work!

SPONSOR A CHILD...

Whether your charity is working to support children, families or pets, you can create a "Sponsor a ___ " (fill in the blank) fundraiser to raise funds for the work you are doing within the community. When you ask supporters to sponsor a specific family, child or pet it is helpful to share a short story of how their regular (i.e. monthly, quarterly) donation is assisting that specific life. For example, if your donor decides to sponsor Erica, a special needs dog; what can you share about the background of this pet? Was she rescued from an abusive situation? What are the pet's needs at this time? How will a regular sponsor help to enhance this pet's life? (Share a photo of the pet alongside the DONATE NOW button on your webpage).

Studies show that we are more likely to donate to one specific family, pet or child versus a large group of the like. Why? Psychologically we want to know that we are helping. We want to know that we are actually making a difference with our donation efforts. If we donate $10 a month to help a family living in a homeless shelter, we know that those dollars matter. It is important to note, if we as individuals donate $10 to help millions of starving children, we begin to wonder if our few dollars really matter. But if an organization requests assistance for a specific child in need, we feel better about our donation as we know it can make a difference for that child.

What is your organization doing on a daily basis? Does your facility house FIV positive felines who have a difficult time finding adoption? Create a sponsor a cat page for those specific cats who you are providing ongoing long-term care. Donors will respond well to regular updates on their sponsored family/pet/child as they become invested in their well-being. This fundraiser works best for charities providing ongoing, regular care to local lives in need.

FOOD DRIVE

Host a food, coat or other type of drive for your charity. Do you need help collecting winter coats for needy children? Or maybe your organization works to provide food donations to families in temporary need of assistance. Make the drive unique and specific to your charity. What item do you need assistance collecting? Will this item make an immediate impact on the lives you are working to assist?

Spreading the word is crucial to this event. Set the date(s). Will you be collecting items for one week, one day or one month? If possible, set up various drop-off locations for donated items. Place matching bins or barrels with your charity's logo at each location and have a volunteer check them often. Hang flyers at local businesses; spread the word on social media and on your website. Write a press release for your local paper; contact your local television news crews and radio hosts. The more people who learn about your drive, the more items you will collect for those in need.

JUST ASK!

Yes, it really is that simple. Don't be afraid to ask! Your organization needs funding to continue your work in the community. Let the community know who you are and what you're doing to make a positive impact and ask for a donation. You can set up a table/booth outside of a high-traffic store (with permission, of course), you can ask to have a booth donated to your charity at local festivals and events and you can even go door to door. There is no harm in asking.

When asking for in-person donations, remember the following:

*Always be respectful and courteous.
*If someone says no, smile and thank them for their time (do not continue to try and "sell" them).
*Offer flyers and business cards for your organization.
*Have a jar of candy or another item that may draw potential donors toward your table/booth.
*Be friendly, smile and maintain an upbeat attitude.
*Be knowledgeable. Know your organization's mission, the direct impact on the local community and be armed with specific stories to share.
*Remind potential donors that even $1 or $5 can make a big difference. Let donors know all donations are appreciated.

GIVINGTUESDAY

Not long ago, the 92nd Street YMCA in New York City and the United Nations Foundation created *GivingTuesday* to focus the holidays on charitable giving. *GivingTuesday* puts the spotlight on charitable causes, the Tuesday after Thanksgiving.

Can *GivingTuesday* help your cause? Yes, absolutely! There is no risk involved and by joining the campaign, you can raise funds and awareness for your group.

How can you participate?

* Share your organization's story and explain the importance of your work. How are you making a difference? Who are you making a difference for?
*Consider creating a **matching campaign**. Work with a partner or major donor who will match all donations you receive from the public on *GivingTuesday*.
*Utilize social media to spread the word. Let everyone know that you are part of the campaign!

Use your favorite online search engine to search successful *GivingTuesday* campaigns for additional ideas.

TELL YOUR STORY

Your organization's story is vital to your overall success. Place a short write-up of your story (no more than a half page) on your 'About Us' website page. Share your story often in conversation and with volunteers, too.

Take a moment to think about it: you have $50 to donate to a local charity. One organization's 'About' website page states:

We want to help. We work full-time jobs but try to help in our spare time. Please donate today.

A second charity's 'About' page is blank.

The third charity's 'About' page shares:

When a battered woman and her two young children found themselves homeless and on the run; Ronnie Jacobs heard their story on the local news and her heart sank. In rural Ramble County there were no resources for battered women at that time. Jacobs wanted better for her community and set out to create a safe haven for women and children in urgent need. In 1998 Jacobs founded *Home-Free,* a non-profit charity that offers temporary housing, resources and assistance for battered women (and children).

Home-Free is appreciative of your support. Every donation directly benefits battered women and children in their plight for survival.

Which charity would you prefer to donate? If you said the third charity, you're like 99% of respondents.

Telling your story will yield both direct and indirect donations to your organization. Whether you are the founder of the organization, an employee, volunteer or supporter, knowing the story behind the WHY of the charity you support is imperative to long-term success.

MISSION

Your mission statement should be clear and concise. It should state who you are and what you do, with brevity. As you develop a mission statement for your organization, you will achieve a heightened understanding of your organization.

How does developing a strong mission statement raise funds? Your mission statement is the backbone of your for-purpose organization. The home page of your website should clearly display your mission statement as well as all pamphlets, brochures, and other marketing materials. Potential supporters want to know who you are and what you do and your mission statement is just the place to let them know.

As with telling your organization's story, a compelling and honest mission statement can do wonders for your charity. An organized and professionally written mission statement is key to attracting and retaining donors.

The importance of a proper mission statement is key to an organization's success. Whether you volunteer, work for or support a charity, if you're working to help raise awareness and funding for that organization, take a moment to review their mission statement. If you have trouble finding the mission statement or if the wording is confusing, outdated or unclear, bring this to the attention of the Board of Directors or the Executive Director of the group. Remember, there is not a one-size-fits-all formula here; but honesty, clarity and brevity are essential to mission statements.

Strong mission statements can yield indirect donations by helping to establish credibility and trustworthiness with your organization.

BOWLING CONTEST

Big Brothers Big Sisters charities are known for their successful *Bowling for Kids* fundraiser events. Any organization, regardless of size, can organize a bowling event. If you're up for the challenge, all ages can enjoy this fun-filled fundraiser.

If you're wondering where to begin, consider the following options:

*Ask your local bowling alley if they will donate or offer a discounted rate on multiple bowling lanes (discuss specific dates and times). Provide an estimated number of participants. If you are a non-profit organization, often facilities will offer group rates or another form of discount.

*If you're not ready to host an event for your organization, ask the bowling alley to donate 20% of the proceeds to your charity / cause on a specific date. (This is a good way to get your feet wet and develop a relationship with the local business if you haven't previously organized a bowling fundraiser).

Regardless of which option you choose, it's important to plan ahead and spread the word. Post flyers, social media posts, posters, newspaper ads and press releases. Consider sending specific invites to local groups and to your loyal supporters.

There are several types of bowling fundraisers you can host. A few examples are listed below:

*Bowling for fun (gather a crowd, enjoy yourselves and all funds raised go to charity).
*Bowl-a-thon (Establish competing teams and see who can play the longest).
*Glow-in-the-Dark Bowling (you can pair this with a theme, such as 80's night).
*Pledge (Have individuals or teams collect donation pledges).

GROW ORGANICALLY

Do good work. Do consistent work. Do honest work. When you follow these three basic rules, amazing things will occur. The work of your organization will promote excitement throughout your local community. The word will spread organically about the work you are doing. Although we are tied to our computers much of the time, humans are still hardwired to connect and communicate. The experiences your organization provides to the local community will spread. When you do good work, people start hearing about it.

While marketing your organization is be helpful, growing organically can yield higher donations in the long run. That is because growing naturally has a greater potential of bringing lifelong donors to your organization.

How do you grow organically? A few ideas (to get you started) are listed below:

*Telling your story.
*Having a strong mission statement.
*Doing good, consistent and honest work.
*Doing what you say you will do *(this is a big one!)*
*Content marketing (i.e. blogging to drive traffic to your website).
*Social Media (consistent posting, informative/helpful posts).
*Establishing an e-mail list.

There isn't a secret formula. Like anything in life, it's about consistent hard work and dedication to the cause--- and letting the public know exactly what you are doing to help your local community.

Growing organically may sound incredibly simple, but it takes patience and persistence to raise funds in this manner. Fundraising may often come indirectly, but in the process you will gain many lifetime donors, supporters and champions to your cause. Don't underestimate the power of this fundraiser. While it's not a specific *event*, it is imperative to your long-term success and credibility.

PHOTOGRAPHS

Do you or a volunteer have a professional camera that can capture hi-resolution photographs? If so, don't miss out on this money-making opportunity for your charity!

If you have a camera and a volunteer you're half way there...

*Simply capture great photos of the work you are doing daily in your community. Share the photos on your website, social media pages, newsletter and press releases. The old saying rings true, "A picture is worth a thousand words".

*Coordinate with a local photographer to attend your fundraiser event. Ask that they donate their services to capture group, couple, pet or family photos for a donation (at the event).

*If you are an animal rescue charity, work with a volunteer photographer to capture beautiful photos of your adoptable and/or special needs pets. Print 8x10 (or larger) photographs and frame. Auction the photographs on your website or at one of your events with proceeds going to your charity.

SOCIAL MEDIA

It's free and it works! When you consistently post on your organization's social media sites, you can build a network of online supporters (that may differ from your in-person donors). Follow the 80/20 rule: focus 80% of your posts on sharing helpful information to your followers and 20% of your posts on the promotion of your charity. (i.e. donate today). Following the 80/20 rule will help your organization gain both credibility and trust from your followers.

If you're following a page on social media, do you want to see posts that provide you with insightful and interesting information or do you want to see "Donate Now!" each day? Putting yourself in your supporter's shoes will help focus your social media posts to gain additional followers now and in the future. As with everything, consistency is the key!

Keep in mind, that even though 80% of your posts will focus on insightful, funny and/or interesting information, you can always include your charity's website address (or link to donate) at the bottom of every post.

What social media avenues should your organization join? That is a question that only you can answer. Join the sites that you or a volunteer have time and energy to maintain in a professional manner (on behalf of your organization). Do you have a volunteer who loves *Pinterest*? Ask them to create a social media page on your charity's behalf and post information to the page daily. Just remember, it's not about how many social media sites you join, it's about growing supporters (and therefore donations!).

As with e-mail lists and mission statements, social media will yield both direct and indirect donations. Keeping professional and consistent posts on your social media sites will garner credibility and trust with your organization, much-needed elements to earning long-term supporters to your cause and your work.

EBAY

The Pay Pal Giving Fund (formerly Mission Fish) is an independent 501(c)3 organization that provides businesses and individuals an easy way to support their favorite causes. A program within the Pay Pal Giving Fund called EBAY Giving Works offers three ways to support your charity.

EBAY Giving Works enables members of the EBAY community to donate to their favorite cause. Sellers can donate a portion from the proceeds of their sale of their item(s) to their favorite charity (from 1-100%). For example, if an individual is selling a vintage necklace on EBAY and designates your charity to receive 50% of the proceeds, your charity will receive that amount when the item sells.

Buyers can also add a donation to their purchase at check-out (designated to a specific non-profit charity).

EBAY Giving Works also allows anyone with a PayPal account to directly donate to their favorite charity with no fees assessed. None! That's a pretty sweet deal.

If your non-profit isn't a part of this no-risk program, it's time to get started now!

ONLINE AUCTION

An online auction can take place on a well-known site, such as EBAY, or you can create your own. Online auctions can yield $500 or more in funds for your charity.

If you choose to utilize EBAY, the key is organization. List your items and set a deadline for sale dates. Then get to work on spreading the word and publicizing your online auction. Let supporters know what type of items they can expect to find, the dates your auction will be running and what project (person, animal, et cetera) the funds raised will be supporting. Getting the word out is essential!

If you decide to create your own online auction fundraiser, check out websites such as *YouCaring* to collect donations. As with any fundraiser, designate a coordinator(s) for the event (someone who is trustworthy, organized and motivated). Plan ahead by collecting items for your event (more items and variety will help boost sales). If you have a lot of small items, consider creating gift baskets to auction. If you create gift baskets, develop a theme for each basket and label the basket with a creative title (i.e. a basket full of bathroom and spa type items could be titled: The Relaxation Basket).

Be sure the winning bidder receives a copy of your charities business card (and a thank you flyer or note) with their item.

BLOG

Compelling and consistent content are non-negotiable for your blog. Writing a blog for your charity is not for everyone. But if you decide to add a blog to your website, make the most of it! Experts recommended that you post to your blog on a consistent schedule (i.e. once a week), allowing your supporters and readers to know when to expect new content. It is just as crucial to stay on topic. If you operate a Food Bank charity for individuals/families in need, keep your blog entries focused on this topic. You can write about where to donate, current fundraisers, sales on specific foods at your local grocery store (if the store is offering a "Buy One, Get One" deal, ask that shoppers donate their "Get One" to your Food Bank). Someone reading your charities blog wants to learn more about *you* and your knowledge about the topic. If you operate a charity that provides temporary housing for the homeless, don't write a blog on your organization's website talking about how to adopt a pet. Stay focused on *your* topic.

How do you write compelling content? Below are a few ideas to get you started:

*Speak with others in your organization. What ideas do they have for interesting (and/or helpful) blog topics?
*Once you've developed (even a small) base of regular readers on your blog, consider asking them what questions they have or what topics they would

like to see you cover on your blog. You can gain a lot of terrific ideas this way!

*The interview: interview an employee or volunteer in your organization. Consider creating a *"Get to Know Us..."* regular occurring blog segment.

*Share what you've learned (or are learning). We all crave knowledge and learning through shared experiences is the best motivator.

*"How to" articles (relating to your focus).

Your blog can also be a great place to share information on your organizations upcoming fundraiser events. While it's not recommended to solely utilize your blog for fundraising promotion, adding blog entries with this content can prove beneficial when you are regularly posting and providing insightful, entertaining and interesting entries to your readers.

How do you write consistent content? Set a schedule and stick to it. If you are in charge of the blog content for your group's website, set a deadline. You can plan ahead and pre-schedule your blog posts, too. Pick a day of the week, for example, and schedule each new post to go live at that time (i.e. Wednesday's at 10 A.M. EST). Consistency is the name of the game when it comes to blogging. We've all stumbled on blogs, reading a great post and hoping for more, only to find that the last time the blogger updated their site was two-years ago (bummer). Stay consistent and earn followers (which often translate into donors and supporters).

At the bottom of every blog post you can include a quick (no more than one or two short sentences) request for donations, with a link to directly donate on your website.

Blogs help your group build credibility and trust. They will yield both direct and indirect donations. Check out *Blogging for Dummies* to learn how to create successful SEO (search engine optimization), drawing readers to your blog (and to your cause).

SKILL SET

Whether your organization has 5 volunteers or 500, it's important to remember that each person has a special talent or skill. Ask employees and volunteers to use their skills to help raise funds for your charity.

Do you have a volunteer who plays the guitar? Ask them to provide group lessons, once a month at your facility, with the class fee going directly to your charity as a donation. Do you know someone who teaches yoga? Why not ask him/her if they will teach a class on behalf of your for-purpose organization. You can host a YOGA IN THE PARK fundraiser. Every participant pays an entry fee to join the 1 or 2 hour session (i.e. $25) and the proceeds are donated to your group.

Invite your supporters, volunteers and employees to utilize their talents and skills to support a great cause. Creating unique fundraisers around skill sets allows your supporters to become a part of your organization (and the events are always a lot of fun).

TUPPERWARE SALE

Do you have a volunteer, employee or supporter who sells Tupperware, MaryKay, ThirtyOne or other items? If so, ask them to donate a portion of the proceeds to your group. Host a one night event to honor your cause (i.e. 30% of sales go to your organization). Set the date, invite everyone you can think of, make it fun and help generate sales! Consider having live music at your event and have appetizers and drinks available for attendees. Often these events are held in someone's home. Make it comfortable and enjoyable.

Be sure to have at least one representative from your group at the event. It's important to have a representative attend to answer questions about the organization. Not only will a portion of the night's proceeds benefit your charity, attendees may also make a direct donation to your organization (in addition to or in lieu of purchasing items).

FLOWER DAY

Pre-sale flowers to a large business or school employees (this fundraiser tends to generate the most interest on Sweetest Day and Valentine's Day). Your volunteers can deliver the flowers to the recipient on the scheduled day. Flower day sales fundraiser's are successful for both large and small organizations. The fundraiser can raise $250 or more.

Be sure to include a personalized card that includes your group's logo and website information.

RELATIONSHIPS

Do not underestimate the power of building relationships. Whether someone donates $5 or $1000 to your group, always thank them for their donation. But don't stop there. Tell them *how* your organization is utilizing their donation. If you can share photos of the specific project in which their funds are benefiting - even better! When you have follow-through, you will generate repeat donors to your cause.

In addition to building relationships with existing donors, don't forget to connect with others. If you're passionate about your cause, you will find yourself sharing your experiences with people who you meet. Without trying to garner donations, you'll be doing so, simply by sharing. It is human nature to connect through stories. When you share your stories and experiences with others, in most cases you will find a point of connection. It's important to remember that you can't fake passion. If you're sharing your experiences (relating to your charity) with the intent of "selling", you won't gain supporters to your cause. But if you're truly excited about the work that your organization is providing to the community, it will reflect in your actions and your words. It's true! Enthusiasm is contagious (and we all know when it's genuine and when it's not).

If you're asking yourself how relationships bring donations, re-read the above paragraph.

BONUS: Read Seth Godin's book, *Permission Marketing: Turning Strangers into Friends and Friends into Customers.*

DODGEBALL TOURNAMENT

Sound fun? It is! Dodgeball isn't just for kids. It's an exciting game where players are separated into two teams. Players on each team throw soft foam balls to try and hit the opposite team, while trying to avoid being hit themselves.

Ask a local school, college or YMCA to rent their gym space to you at a discounted rate (or better yet, donate it) for a dodgeball tournament fundraiser night.

Participants pay a fee to play (this is how you raise funds for your cause). Consider selling shirts or other apparel with your charity logo and the name of your dodge ball tournament, to raise additional funds for your organization.

Offering a pre-registration option helps your fundraising coordinator plan ahead with scheduling and equipment.

VIDEO GAME MARATHON

Host a video game marathon to raise funds for your charity. Charge an entry fee (proceeds go directly to your organization). *PayPal* is a website that assists you in clearly keeping track of donations (www.paypal.com).

Additional tips:

*Create an experience at your event (make it fun)!
*Select games with a clear start and finish.
*Consider asking participants to gain sponsors (donating a set amount for every hour played).
*Create a schedule for your event on Ustream.TV (do this well in advance of your event).

SWIMMING LESSON

Collaborate with your local public pool, country club or YMCA to offer a day of swimming lessons. Target a specific skill set and/or age group for the lesson. Plan a date, create an intriguing title for your event and start spreading the word.

When working with a local facility, ask that they donate a percentage of the proceeds to your charity (i.e. Your group receives 50% of the registration fee).

Another pool related fundraiser idea: hold a treading water contest or swim-athon.

SPECIAL NOTE: Be certain instructors are certified. Discuss liability waivers with the facility prior to your event.

CRAFT SALE

You don't have to be crafty to host a craft sale!

Location
Depending on the size and expected attendance for your event, there are a variety of locations you might consider for hosting your craft sale fundraiser:

*Country club building
*School gymnasium
*Church
*Large outdoor parking lot

Items
Be sure to have more than enough tables to display your items. It's also important to plan ahead with chairs. Volunteers working at the event will appreciate your preparation on this front. Other items to prepare:

*Change
*Ability to accept credit card payments for items sold
*Price tags
*Inventory sheet (or other form of organization)
*Designated check-out area
*Promotional items (i.e. flyers, business cards) for your charity

Obtain craft items well in advance of your event. Utilize your e-mail list, blog, and social media to request craft donations for the event. Set a deadline for the collection of donated items. Will you pick up the items or are delivered directly to your organization?

Craft sales can raise substantial donations when you offer plenty of items, spread the word about your event and host your event in an easily accessible location.

RECIPE BOOKS

Reach out to supporters, volunteers and others in your organization to collect favorite recipes. Consider designing sections for appetizers, finger foods, main dishes, and desserts. If you don't have a large group to network with, try utilizing a *CrowdFunding* website to locate recipe ideas (www.crowdfunding.com). Once you have a substantial amount of recipes, compile a hard copy of your collected recipes to sell. Set your selling price and get to work. Begin selling recipe books online through your website and social media. They can also be sold at many of your events: take them with you everywhere you go!

50/50 RAFFLE

You can offer a 50/50 raffle at every fundraiser event
you host. You can also offer the raffle online. This is
an easy to operate fundraiser that you can host any
time of the year. Whether you have one volunteer or
many, you can't go wrong with a 50/50 raffle.

If you're hosting your 50/50 raffle at an event, you
can increase overall funds raised and increase interest
from attendees. Get started by utilizing the ideas
below:

*The prize of the 50/50 draw will be half of the
amount collected from ticket sales.
*Set a clear start and end date/time for the raffle.
*When you purchase your roll of raffle tickets, be
sure the tickets have two sections that can be torn off
(showing a unique serial number). Place one half of
the raffle ticket in the raffle bucket, the other half will
be given to the donor.
* Announce the winner at a pre-determined time and
be sure to let participants know if raffle winners must
be present.
*Price tickets between $1-10/each to encourage
multiple ticket purchases.

JEANS DAY

Work with a local school or business to create a designated Jeans Day. This can occur once a year or once a month. Ask the business to allow employees to wear jeans on a pre-determined Friday. The catch is, if the employees indulge in wearing jeans, they donate $5 to your cause.

Create professional flyers and spread the word. Decide who will collect the $5 from employees on the designated day. And let employees know how their $5 will benefit the local community. Design a catchy slogan for the event to capture even more donors (i.e. *Get your Jeans On! Raising Awareness for Autism*).

You can also utilize the same concept for Hat Day, Pajama Day, et cetera.

COOK OFF

Choose a specific food and let the games begin! Find local community members who wish to enter their food item (i.e. apple pie), set a location and date for the event and spread the word. Attendees purchase tickets to attend and taste the food.

Decide ahead of time how you will determine a winner. Will you have a panel of judges? Will you accept votes from attendees? Be sure to create a rules and regulations sheet (and bring copies).

What prizes will you offer, and how many?

Work with volunteers to solicit the prize donations. Volunteers can also help with ticket sales. On the day of the event you will need volunteers to assist with welcoming guests, collecting attendance fees, announcing the winners, et cetera.

Cook offs often generate $500 or more. Plan ahead, stay organized and enjoy!

BIRTHDAY PLEDGES

Happy Birthday to you…Happy Birthday to you…

Create a birthday pledge program for your cause.
Utilizing social media can greatly enhance your
success. How does it work? Create a page on your
website (and a flyer that you post regularly on your
social media pages) for birthday pledges. Let your
supporters know that when they donate $5 or more in
honor of a loved one's birthday, your
organization/cause will e-mail (or mail) that person
special birthday card and post a birthday
message/photo on your most popular social media
page.

If you would like to take this idea a step further, you
can offer to create a specific page on your website for
an individual's birthday. For example, the page can
state that *Hanna George* is raising funds for your
charity. Her goal is to raise $200 by a specific date.
Creating a page for the birthday individual is
beneficial as it allows you to provide a specific
donation link to Hanna that she can share with her
own group of friends and family to support the cause.

SPA NIGHT

Find volunteers to give five-minute back and/or shoulder massage and a mani-pedi for a set donation. Secure a location; set a date/time and send your invitations.

This event is easy to facilitate and can even be hosted in your home if you have a large enough space.

To take a different spin on this fundraiser, you can bring the spa to work. Collaborate with a local business to schedule a date/time to bring your "spa" treatment (volunteers) to the workplace. This could take place on a Friday during lunch hours (11 AM – 1PM).

AMAZON SMILE

Sign up for an Amazon Smile account and let your supporters know! Once your supporters have signed up, every time they use Amazon Smile to purchase an item, Amazon will donate to your organization (at no cost to the buyer or you). This program is for 501(c)3 organizations (go to: *smile.amazon.com* to get started).

Set up your account today, spread the word and let the shopping begin!

ENTERTAINMENT COUPON BOOKS

Entertainment Coupon Books work with schools, churches, community groups, sports teams, charities and non-profit organizations. There are no upfront costs and your cause can earn up to 40% of the proceeds from your sales. Entertainment Coupon Books also offer free shipping to your organization.

There are no upfront payments involved with this fundraiser (you pay them after your sales). Even better, the company has a new mobile app that provides access to local editions.

FLAG FOOTBALL TOURNAMENT

Host a flag football tournament in your local community, to raise awareness and funds for your group. Done correctly, this fundraiser can yield upwards of $1,000 in donations.

One successful event worked with teams consisting of 7-15 co-ed players each. Teams competed in a 7-on-7 flag tournament officiated by trained referees. Games lasted 25 minutes with double elimination. (Guarantee each team at least two games. Additional – and optional – activities were available between games).

Charge a participation donation (entry fee). Raise additional funds by inviting spectators and charging a General Admission fee.

If you want to go further: have food and drinks available to players. Provide dinner with each ticket purchased and prizes to the top three teams.

As with all events, plan ahead and stay organized. Now get ready to play for a good cause!

CAKE WALK

Find supporters to donate cakes. Ten cakes is the minimum recommendation (but remember, the more cakes, the more fun). Depending on the number of attendees, develop a circle for participants - generally with twenty-spots. Tape your numbers around your designated circle. Place copies of these same numbers on a sheet of paper and place them in a bowl or bag.

Raise funds for your cause by selling tickets for each turn in the cake walk. Cake donations make the expenses for this event minimal. You can also add a cake walk onto another event you are hosting (to boost the funds raised).

Ask participants to walk in the circle as the music plays. When you shut the music off, each participant claims the cake closest to them. The coordinator will then pull a number from the bowl or bag. The person standing next to the number that was pulled from the bag is the winner. At that time, the winner can choose their favorite cake to take. Continue playing until every cake has a winner!

Have fun with this event. Invite participants to walk, skip or dance in the circle (while the music is playing).

ORNAMENT FUNDRAISER

Set up a festive tree during the holidays. You can set the tree up in the entrance or lobby of your facility. If you do not own a facility, consider asking a local business or store to allow the set-up of your fundraising tree.

Create a sign that says *"Add an ornament for a great cause!"* Create an ornament that represents your charity/cause (i.e. if you are an animal rescue, create ornaments that look like cats and dogs). Every time someone donates $5 to your organization, they write their name on one of the ornaments and hang it on the tree. The goal is to fill the tree before the holidays end.

FLOWER BULB SALE

Flower Power Fundraising
(www.flowerpowerfundraising.com) allows your organization to earn up to a 50% profit on flower bulb sales. You can host an online only or a door-to-door sales event for your group. The company shares, *"Just this past year, we helped schools, churches, sports teams and many other groups from across the country raise millions of dollars with our face-to-face catalog and online fundraising programs, and this year, we'd like to help you too."*

Dutch Mill Bulbs also offers a fundraising program for schools, churches and other groups (www.dutchmillbulbs.com).

Selling flower bulbs is a great way to spread the word about your organization and raise funds!

Visit the above company's websites and/or use your favorite search engine to locate a company you will enjoy working with for your groups flower bulb fundraiser.

INKJET RECYCLING

Companies like *Recycle for Charity* (www.recycle4charity.com) provide a safe place for individuals and companies to donate empty used laser toner, used inkjet printer cartridges, and cell phones. You can help the environment and your favorite charity at the same time! The company's Recycle 4 Fundraising program allows you to collect empty items (mentioned above) and raise cash for your cause. The company provides free bulk pick-up of items, flyers and shipping labels. Your job is to sign up your charity, spread the word, collect donations and arrange for a pick up; and in return, you receive a cash donation!

NOTE: There are several additional companies that provide this type of fundraiser. Please use your favorite search engine to compare companies and find one that you wish to work with for your group's inkjet recycling fundraiser.

ALUMNIUM RECYCLING

Collect aluminum cans and recycle for cash. You can set up a bin for aluminum recycling outside of your building or in your lobby. You may also consider partnering with a local store. Ask your local Walmart or Target store if you can place a large aluminum recycling bin in their employee area; stop in to collect the cans once a week. Take the aluminum to your local recycling center and donate the cash to the charity/cause of your choice.

GUESSING JARS

You can add this to an existing event to raise additional donations, or you can host a guessing jar fundraiser online (via your social media sites). Simply fill a jar with candy (M&M's work well) or another item and have participants guess the number of items in the jar.

If you're hosting the fundraiser in person, have each participant record their guess on a sheet near the jar (so that no one has the same guess). Set an ending date and time. When time is called, the participant who guessed closest to the number wins the jar of items and/or a prize.

Charge each participant $1 per guess to raise funds for your group. Be sure that your jar is attractive (consider adding a bow) to draw more interest.

Ideas of other items to fill guessing jars:

*Shells
*Legos
*Corks
*Beads
*Coins
*Marbles
*Golf tees
*Pebbles

KARAOKE NIGHT

Hosting a karaoke night is an entertaining way to raise funds for your cause. Depending on the number of attendees, you can host this fundraiser in your home (if you have a large space) or in a rented space.

Charging an admission fee allows you to raise funds for your organization. This event works well when hosted on a regular basis (i.e. once a month or quarter).

Points to remember:

*Determine your location (is there a cost?).
*Set the date/time of your event (with this be a reoccurring fundraiser?).
*Rent (or purchase) a karaoke machine and music.
*Have food/drinks available.

Other variations of this fundraiser include:

*Collaborating with a large business to host Karaoke Friday (i.e. once a month) in the workplace, during lunch hours.

*At your event, host a competition or a sing-a-thon. Provide a prize to the winner and runner-up.

PIE THROW

There are several variations of this interactive fundraiser. You can add this event to an existing fundraiser or host it independently.

A) Host a pie throwing contest. Use a large open space and have a line drawn for participants to stand. Participants receive three pies for each paid entry. See who can throw their pie the furthest. The overall winner receives a prize.

B) Ask your Executive Director or group leader to participate (this may take some begging). This version of the pie throw fundraiser is often referred to as "Pie in the Face." Set a goal for the amount of funds you wish to raise at this event and let the fun begin! Participants donate for each pie they want to throw at the leaders face (establish a line from which they make their attempted throws).

You can raise additional funds at this event by offering the option for individuals to sponsor a throw at the established individual(s).

POT LUCK NIGHT

Host a pot luck night event once a year or once a month and you'll bring in ample funds for your charity, group or school. Ask attendees to donate the amount they would have spent going out to lunch to your charity. To add additional appeal, consider creating a theme for each pot luck event. Invite others in your organization to host these events, too.

Pot luck fundraisers are a great way to bring everyone together to support a great cause.

Consider adding a raffled gift basket to your event. Choose one attendee at random to win the basket at the end of the night.

One group charged $20 per family to attend and asked everyone to bring a dish.

Bring an Entree - If your last name begins with A-H
Bring an Appetizer - If your last name begins with I-P
Bring a Salad - If your last name begins with Q-Z

Make the event your own and most of all have a good time while raising funds!

READ-A-THON

Websites like *Learn2Earn* (www.learn2earn.org) make it easy to host a read-a-thon for your school or cause. The site allows participants to log reading time and your group can earn up to 85% of all pledges received (children read books, families locate sponsors). Hosting a read-a-thon online is a great way to reach a wide audience.

Read-a-thons work great for schools and youth groups.

If you decide to host an in-person read-a-thon event, designate a space and a start and end time. Have a volunteer capture photos and short videos throughout the fundraiser (with permission) and share on social media. Sharing live feed from your event can help gain additional pledges and direct donations to your group.

Consider creating a small thank you gift to read-a-thon participants (i.e. bookmark with your groups logo).

SPAGHETTI DINNER

Get your noodles ready! Hosting a spaghetti dinner for your charity is a great way to draw attention and raise funds for your cause. Choose a venue, and then set a date and time for your event. When you host an annual event, if attendees have a good time, they will come back year after year (often bringing additional friends and family).

When planning your event, examine the following:

*Will you rent a space for your event? Are you able to receive a discount on the space? Is the location easily accessible? Does your location offer ample parking?
*Will your volunteers cook the food or will you hire a caterer?
*Will you offer alcohol? Cash bar?
*Will you require attendees to pre-register?
*How much you will charge each guest? What do they get for the price of their ticket?
*How will you promote your event?
* What is your profit margin on ticket sales?

Consider pairing your spaghetti dinner with a silent auction event, 50/50 raffle, guessing jar and/or trivia night, to add extra pizzazz.

PLANT SALE

This event can take some planning, but can *grow* into a rewarding fundraiser for your group. Plant seeds in flat trays. Transfer to paper cups for individual sales. Place a photo (and short write-up) of the adult plant next to the infant plants.

Have a garden reference book available for buyers to reference additional plant details on the day of your sale. Keep plants watered (don't let them look droopy).

Another way to garner additional interest in your plant sale fundraiser is to offer a raffle of a gardener's basket. You can sell individual tickets for a chance to win, or you can give a free ticket to anyone who purchases five or more plants. A gardener's basket might include: *seeds, towels, gloves, watering can.*

ST. PATTY'S DAY TAXI SERVICE

Bring a dash of good luck to your organization. Ask a local taxi service to donate 10% of St. Patty's Day sales to your charity. (Or, you can pass flyers around for your fundraiser and ask the taxi service to donate a set percentage of sales to your organization, for each *flyer* received.)

If you're highly motivated, another option is to gather volunteers and create a taxi service offered on St. Patty's Day and the following day. How do you create your own service? Work with qualified volunteers in your organization; volunteers drive your taxi service, allowing proceeds to go directly to your charity (Ensure that proper checks are in place prior to operating this program). Operating this fundraiser on an annual basis will allow your event to grow organically and fruitfully. Hosting a St. Patty's Day Taxi Service is a great way to raise funds for your organization and keep people and local roads safe during the holiday.

STAIR CLIMB

Promote great health through physical exercise and raise money for your charity/cause! When you host this fundraiser as an annual event, you will gain a growing crowd (and growing funds, to boot).

Coordinate with a local business to utilize their stairs on your event day. Decorate landings, have plenty of water and snacks available for participants. If you can find a local band to volunteer to play during the event, this adds even more pizzazz to your event.

How many flights of stairs will you have participants climb? How will you indicate the finish? Who will time the event?

Some events have participants run up to one mile prior to beginning the stair climb. The choice is yours. Make the event unique to your cause and start spreading the word!

Another version of this fundraiser is a Climb-a-Thon. Set a time (i.e. four-hours) and see who can achieve the most climbs in that time frame. Offer a prize to the top three finishers.

NOTE: Be sure to have participants sign a liability waiver prior to participation. As with any physical event, it is good practice to have medical professionals available.

WRIST BANDS

Customize wrist band bracelets with your organization's name, tag line and/or logo and start selling! Not only can this fundraiser bring in additional funds to your group, it will also help spread awareness to the great work you are doing in the community.

There are countless websites that offer silicone wrist bands for fundraisers (they will custom design for your group). Use your favorite search engine to locate a company. Many companies will offer your group 40% or more of the proceeds.

SPELL S-U-C-C-E-S-S

It's spell-a-thon time! Host this fundraiser with
children, adults or both. Ask each participant to
collect pledges for the number of words they spell
correctly. Provide (donated) prizes to the top three
winners. You may also want to consider offering a
prize for each age group, depending on how your
event is structured.

Determine a location, date and time for your event
and start spreading the word. Provide rule sheets and
pledge forms to participants.

Get creative with donated prizes for the winners (i.e.
spa package, movie night themed basket). Often, the
bigger the prize, the larger crowd you will draw to
your event.

SMOOTHIE STAND

Try a different twist on the lemonade stand. Host a smoothie stand and raise much needed funds for your charity or cause. Open smoothie stands outside of your building on hot summer days or you can pair them with another fundraiser event (i.e. rummage sale, stair climb).

Consider offering your *'Smoothie's for a Cause'* every Friday (throughout June and July, for example). Smoothies are a great way to bring in additional funds for your cause and bring smiles to both existing and new supporters.

Smoothie stands have low overhead and are easy to operate.

GOLD RUSH

Strike gold for your cause! Gather a group of supporters/volunteers. Everyone asks friends, family and co-workers to donate old jewelry that they no longer wear. Your organization then turns in the gold for cash (donated directly to your charity).

If you are a 501(c)3 organization, be prepared to offer donation receipts (for tax purposes) to your donors. This can add additional incentive for individuals to donate.

Another variation of this fundraiser is to collaborate directly with a jewelry store. Ask the jewelry store to offer your group 50% of the proceeds from all gold jewelry items sold to them during a day or week period of time.

BUY A MEAL

Ask supporters to donate a specific amount of funds or a meal. With this fundraiser, if you are asking for funds, let potential donors know exactly how your organization will utilize the funds. For example:

Donate $12 to provide a day of food
for one child in need

There are a many variations for this fundraiser, depending on your cause or organization's mission. If you operate or volunteer for a Food Pantry, ask supporters to donate homemade meals during the month of January, for example. Homemade meals will then be distributed to recipients of the Food Pantry.

Another variation of this fundraiser involves collaborating with a local restaurant. Ask the restaurant (for a one week period, for example) to support your cause. Ask restaurant employees to set out a donation jar at the check-out counter and to ask every guest if they would like to donate $1 towards a meal for homeless families (or pets) in your local area.

YANKEE CANDLE SALES

Not only do they smell great, but we all know and trust the brand! Yankee Candle sales are a great no-risk way to raise money for your organization. Even better, you earn 40% of the profit from sales.

Yankee Candle provides a catalog to your group. You generate sales and collect funds. The items are shipped to you (each individually wrapped, per buyer), and you distribute. Yankee Candle offers both Spring and Fall fundraisers.

Why wait? Every sale you make benefits your cause and your supporters receive quality products that they can enjoy themselves or give as gifts.

Contact Yankee Candle:
www.yankeecandlefundraising.com

GRAB BAGS

Host a grab bag fundraiser at your facility, school or church – or along with another fundraiser event. You can also offer a grab bag fundraiser if your group has a booth at a local craft bizarre.

The grab bag fundraiser is exactly what it sounds like: grab bags full of different items. Paper lunch bags work great for this fundraiser. Charge a set fee for grab bags (i.e. $5 per bag).

There are a lot of options as to what to include in grab bags. Prior to your event, ask for donations of items (i.e. gift cards, candy) to fill your grab bags. Include a flyer or business card in every grab bag, encouraging individuals to visit your website and social media pages.

A few ideas for items to place in grab bags:

*Candy
*Gift card
*Soaps
*Lotion(s)
*Book(s)
*Keychain
*Shirt
*Wrist band/bracelets
*Toys
*Candle

PUMP IT UP!

Gas stations are popular places. The U.S. Energy Information Administration reports, "In 2013, about 134.51 billion gallons (or 3.20 billion barrels) of gasoline were consumed in the United States, a daily average of about 368.51 million gallons (or 8.77 million barrels)." Gas stations are generating a lot of daily revenue and your organization can benefit. Collaborate with a local gas station for one day. Ask the local gas station if your volunteers can serve as gas station attendants for the day (set specific hours). Volunteers will then offer to pump gas and clean windshields for everyone who visits the gas station during those hours.

It is important to remember, not everyone who comes to the gas station will utilize your volunteers. However, many will. Volunteers can ask for a $5 donation to your organization when they pump gas and/or clean windshields.

Ask volunteers to wear matching shirts with your organizations logo clearly displayed on the front. Provide every client who utilizes your volunteers/donates to your charity, with a flyer or card with your organizations information. Have plenty of change available and have visible, easy to read signs directing people to your volunteers.

CHAIR-ITY FUNDRAISER

Paint wooden chairs in fun patterns with your volunteers. Once you have a large number of painted/decorated chairs, host a CHAIR-ity event to sell the chairs, with proceeds going directly to your organization. Pair Chair-ity events with other fundraisers (i.e. rummage sale) or held on their own. As with all events, be sure your fundraiser is held in an easily accessible location with ample parking.

Get creative! Paint chairs solid colors, multi-colors or cover them with polka dots. Remember, the more chairs you offer for sale, the more funds you can raise for your cause.

CALENDAR SALES

Work with a local or online company to create professional calendars for your organization. If you volunteer for an animal rescue organization, for example, create a 12-month, full-color calendar that feature photographs of rescued pets and pets awaiting adoption. Include a brief write-up at the bottom of each month's photo that describes the specific pet needing adoption.

Calendar sales are a great way to raise both funds and awareness to your organization. When your organization offers calendar sales year after year, you will build a steady, loyal stream of supporters who will continue to purchase your new calendars.

FACE PAINTING

Face painting is not just for kids! If you or a volunteer from your organization enjoy painting, consider hosting a face painting event to raise funds for your cause. Hold this event in conjunction with another fundraiser or on its own. Or you may consider asking a local store (i.e. Walmart, Kroger) or the city pool if you can set up a booth for face painting outside of their doors. This can help drive in additional spur-of-the-moment traffic to your fundraiser. To add consistency to your event (and to help you raise even more funds), consider hosting your face painting booth every Friday from 2-6PM, at the same location, during the month of June, for example.

Be sure to provide a sample of the items you can paint on faces. Offer two to four options (i.e. star, heart, etc). Ask for a donation for every face painted.

CARE PACKAGES

Care packages are a great way to gather donations during the holidays or any other time of year. Offer to deliver a care package to a loved one for specified donation. You can set different amounts for different package sizes. Give a creative name to each care package offered to drum up additional interest. For example, BOX OF SUNSHINE. Charge $25. The gift box is filled with tissues, bath salts and candles, from your organization. There are a large variety of boxes you can create (and you can create them around various themes). Start with one, and see how it works for your organization. You can always add additional care package options to your fundraiser.

When a supporter orders a BOX OF SUNSHINE, for example, what is the typical delivery time? Timing will be essential, as many people may utilize your care package fundraiser for get well packages (or for other occasions).

Offer this fundraiser during either the December holiday month or year-round.

MARCH MADNESS

Although the fundraiser doesn't need to be held in March, it can work well in conjunction with the popular basketball tournament.

How it works: Set a goal of 100 people and ask each person to donate $25. Every day during the month of March, draw a name from the 50 paid entrants. The name drawn wins $25. But when a name is drawn on Friday, that entrant wins $50.

You bring in: 100 x $25 = $2500 income.

Payout 27 days at $25 = 675 and the payout for 4 days at $50 =200

*Your income of $2500 minus the prize money of $875 = **$1625 Profit***

*Source: NASCAR Foundation

Announce the winning names each day on your social media pages. This is a great way to gain additional "likes" on your page and to locate additional supporters for your cause.

CHEER CLINIC

Work with your local university and ask cheerleaders to host a one-day clinic for future cheerleaders. Consider offering sessions based on age. For example, offer a morning clinic for children, age six to eight. In the afternoon offer a second clinic for age nine to twelve. The following day you can offer your clinic for ages thirteen and up.

In addition to collaborating with local university cheerleaders, you will need to establish a location for your event (i.e. high school gymnasium).

The clinic can teach basic cheerleading skills. You can also offer group sessions. For example, have your cheerleading clinic participants rotate between four group sessions (each session focuses on a different skill and provides a different cheer coach).

Charge an entry fee to the event (a percentage of the fee is then donated to your organization).

COLLECTION JARS AT LOCAL BUSINESSES

Create professional and appealing donation jars for your cause. Ask to set your donation jar out at several local businesses. Set the donation jar near the register and ask employees to encourage their visitors to donate to your local cause. Stop in the store once a week to collect donations from the jar.

Consider hanging a poster or flyer for your organization (and to highlight the donation jar at the counter) on the door of the business.

NOTE: Color flyers will garner more attention, often netting higher donations.

BAD TALENT CONTEST

Once you've secured a location for your event, it's time to have fun! A bad talent contest is exactly that: displaying bad talents. Have you been told you're a horrible singer? This is the perfect opportunity to sing out of tune in front of a crowd – all while helping to raise funds for a great cause. Other ideas can include bad dance routines, attempting to state a riddle ten times in a row at top speed, et cetera.

Charge $1 for each participant and charge an entry fee of $5. You can easily pair this event with other fundraisers to bring in even more donations. This is a low-budget fundraiser that can help raise much-needed donations.

WARNING: This event tends to involve a lot of laughter!

SPEED DATING

Charge a $20 registration fee (or any amount you choose) and play matchmaker for local singles ages 21 and older. Determine a location, create flyers, spread the word and get to work. It is helpful to have a specific number of pre-registered bachelors prior to announcing open registration. For example, if you have 20 registered eligible bachelors – share a few quotes or a photo of a few of them on your fundraising website page and encourage others to join your event. Remind everyone that they are speed dating for a great cause, too!

There are a variety of ways to operate this event. For example, you can offer two-minute sessions. Males stay at their assigned tables. Females rotate every time the bell rings to indicate that two-minutes have passed.

You can add additional flare to your event by setting rules (i.e. set specific off-limit topics– for example, careers).

PAINT THE TOWN

Gather a group of volunteers and visit local neighborhoods. Go door-to-door with flyers for your fundraiser (be sure flyers clearly state your organizations name and contact information) and ask residents if they would like you to paint their house number on the street curb – for a donation.

If the homeowner agrees, use a cardboard cut-out to paint a black rectangular background on the curb. Once it dries, paint the house number (using a stencil) in reflective paint.

SPECIAL NOTE: Prior to your fundraiser, find out if your city requires permits. Be sure to follow all city and / municipality guidelines by checking with your local municipality and the local police and fire departments.

BE MY VALENTINE

Two weeks prior to Valentine's Day, begin spreading the word about your BE MY VALENTINE fundraiser. For a $5 donation, send a Valentine's card from your organization to the designated recipient. Choose to utilize e-cards or snail mail cards. This is a great way for your supporters to donate to a worthy cause and send their love to someone they care about.

TARGET

Target's School Fundraising program has helped more than 114,000 schools pay for computers, playground equipment, field trips and uniforms for students whose families couldn't afford them.

How can you get involved? Target offers a TargetVisa or TargetGuestCard. Everytime a purchase is made in store or online using one of the above payment methods, Target will donate ½ - 1% to the K-12 school of your choice.

NOTE: Visit Target.com and click on the Target Guest Card link (under Financial Services), for additional information.

P.J.'S AT SCHOOL!

Hold this fundraiser once a year or once a month - the choice is yours! Collaborate with your school district to host a P.J. DAY. Students pay $1.00 (or any amount you have determined appropriate) on P.J. DAY and they can wear their pajamas to school. Each classroom teacher collects the funds for his/her students.

You may consider offering a "pre-sale" and allow parents and teachers to donate to the PJ fund. If a teacher donates $2 to the fund, he/she will be given two-free P.J. DAY passes (one for each dollar donated). The teacher can then use their free pass as a reward for a well-behaved student, for example.

To take this fundraiser a step further, you may consider hosting a pajama contest during lunch period (i.e. coziest pajamas) and offer small prizes for the winners in each category.

MOM-O-GRAMS

This fundraiser works great for Mother's Day, but can also be re-titled and hosted on other important days such as St. Patrick's Day or Valentine's Day.

Work with a local company that will provide a discount to your group on corsages (or if you have volunteers who can make them - that's even better!). Collect orders and funds for the corsages in advance. Create an order sheet that provides detailed information on each corsage ordered (i.e. full name, address, telephone number, delivery date). Offer to add small personalized notecards to the corsage delivery (i.e. note from a daughter to her mom).

Deliver your corsages the night before the event/holiday (i.e. Mother's Day, Valentine's Day). When you deliver the corsage, also give the recipient a flyer or business card for your cause/organization.

JUMP-A-THON

Jump for _____! *(Fill in the blank with your cause)*.
Create a buzz: hang flyers, posters, create a webpage,
spread the word on social media. Get the word out
and get started. Participants ask for pledges for how
many minutes they can jump rope. Collected pledges
benefit your cause/charity.

The participants actual jumping can take place in a
large gymnasium, with other jumpers. Or jumpers can
video themselves jumping and post on your
organizations social media page to directly thank their
donors (and possibly generate additional
pledges/donors for their efforts).

BALL DROP!

Collect and sell used golf balls for $5-15 each (your choice). Set a date and time to have the balls dumped from a front-end loader, crane or any other creative option. Drop all the golf balls at one time near a designated pin or hole. The owner of the ball closest to the designated pin will win a predetermined portion of the profit (i.e. 50%).

HOW TO SELL: Number each ball. When someone purchases a ball, don't give the ball to them; give them a receipt with the number of *their* ball. Keep a well-organized chart (listing names and ball numbers).

SPECIAL NOTE: Have a large volunteer clean-up crew ready to collect golf balls after the winner is announced.

REVERSE RAFFLE

Pass out free raffle tickets to your supporters and allow them to sell back their ticket for a $10 donation. Why would they want to sell their ticket back? Because everyone you give a raffle ticket to is entered in a drawing (on a given date/time) and chosen names from the raffle will be asked to do something embarrassing (i.e. dance in front of everyone). This works well as an add-on to a fundraiser event. It also works well when hosted at a school or anywhere you have a large gathering of people.

CHARADES

Act it out, guess, laugh and raise funds for your charity! There are a variety of ways to host charades as a fundraiser event.

The Gale Recovery Center in New Jersey invited teams of five. Teams paid a fee of $100 to participate. Each team had ten-minutes to guess charades from their teammates. Prizes were given to the top three teams.

Plan ahead. Seek donated prizes from local businesses prior to your event (i.e. restaurant gift cards). Plan your categories in advance (i.e. books, songs, television shows, music, movies).

This can be a stand-alone event or paired with another fundraiser. Host the event in someone's home, your organizations facility, a school gymnasium or any large area.

X MARKS THE SPOT

You need a hill and golf balls for this fundraiser. Contact a local driving range and ask for a donation of used golf balls for the event. On the day of your event, clearly mark a spot at the bottom of the hill (this is the "goal" area). Making a large "X" with spray paint works well for marking the spot.

Sell a chance to win for $5-10 each (you decide the prize). Assign a number to each ball (keep an organized chart of numbers). On the date of your event, the individual who purchased the golf ball is blindfolded and they toss their ball down the hill.

The three balls that come the closest to the marked area win a prize.

Offering a cash prize is a great way to draw a larger crowd to this event!

MOVIE NIGHT

Host a movie night in a large room. Having access to a large screen TV is helpful. Determine the location, date and time of your event. Also determine the movie that will be played. Charge an admission price to attend. Attendees will be able to view the movie and enjoy refreshments.

Other variations of this fundraiser:

A) Provide the movie for free and ask for donations.
B) Provide the movie for free and sell refreshments.

Allow time for socializing before and after the movie. Having a knowledgeable representative from your organization attend the event can be helpful, too. Your organizations representative/leader may want to share a brief thank you and/or a story of how donations help the cause, prior to the movie.

EAT FOR A CAUSE

Work with a local restaurant to support your cause. Ask the manager to donate 10% of the restaurant's profits on a designated night (i.e. Monday, 2/23 from 5-8PM). In return, you will drive more business to their restaurant by encouraging your supporters to attend. Restaurant managers/owners are generally more receptive to working with local causes when the suggested time frame is during a time slot where they can use more business.

The larger the crowd you draw, the more profit you can earn for your organization. Create a professional flyer and spread the word.

BOARD GAME TOURNAMENT

It's competition time! Collect an entry fee of $10 per person and provide prizes to the top three individuals or teams (depending on how you structure the event). HINT: Use donated items as prizes (i.e. restaurant gift cards, spa package). Set the date, time and location of your event. Provide a list of prizes and a rule sheet.

What game will you utilize for your event? Games that tend to work well for this type of fundraising tournament are: Uno, Twister, Battleship, Catch Phrase and Scrabble.

Consider hosting this event regularly. Holding the event once a month will draw a larger crowd and additional funds for your cause (you may want to host the event once a month and feature a different game each month).

You can also raise additional funds by selling refreshments or offering a 50/50 raffle at your event.

HOLIDAY CAROLING

Gather a group of supporters and head out for holiday caroling. How do you raise funds for your organization? Announce your holiday caroling fundraiser well in advance. Determine a schedule for which area (i.e. specific streets, zip code, town) you will visit. Supporters can request your group to carol at their home or on their street for a $5 – 10 donation.

Arm volunteers with flyers for your organization. Not only will you be having fun and raising funds for a worthy cause, but you'll be spreading the word and possibly gaining long-term donors as you sing through the night.

HOLIDAY LIGHT REMOVAL

When the holidays are over, it's time to take down the decorations. Yes, that includes holiday lights. Gather a group of volunteers to provide an annual holiday light removal service in your community. Send out mailers, post flyers and spread the word on social media. We all lead busy lives and taking down the holiday lights is not always at the top of our *to do* list. When your organization offers to provide this service for a set donation to your charity, residents will be eager to utilize your service knowing that they have help with a chore they've been dreading and their funds are going to great local cause.

SHOVELING DRIVEWAYS

It may sound basic, but it works! Designate volunteers in various neighborhoods to shovel snow from driveways for a donation to your organization. Provide volunteers with flyers for your group. Spread the word in advance or simply go door-to-door when bad weather strikes, and explain that you are shoveling for a cause. Depending on the amount of volunteers participating, your organization can raise $500 or more.

Request a $20 donation for each driveway shoveled. If you have 5 sets of volunteers who each shovel just 5 driveways in one day, you will bring in $500 for your cause (and you'll get a great workout)!

DART TOURNAMENT

This is exactly how it sounds. Select a location, date and time for the event and throw your darts! Have prizes on hand for the top three winners. Secure donated prizes prior to the event (i.e. gift cards, event tickets).

To raise additional funds, consider adding a 50/50 raffle to your event. You can also sell refreshments.

GUIDED NATURE HIKE

Work with your local nature preserve or organize a hike on your own. Select a trail (anywhere from ¼ to a full mile in distance). If you're working with your local nature preserve, they will appoint a trail guide to educate hikers during the walk. If you're organizing this event on your own, be sure to appoint a trail guide/leader who is both enthusiastic and knowledgeable about nature. Trail guides will point out a variety of highlights during the walk, such as: birds (naming the type of bird and several facts about them), trees, as well as debunking general myths. Trail guides should be able to answer questions from attendees, as well.

When you collaborate with your local nature preserve, ask that they charge a fee to attendees and donate a percentage to your cause.

Be sure to inform attendees to dress properly, prior to attending the event (i.e. proper shoes). As the organizer of this fundraiser event, it is a good idea to bring a backpack with several drinks, snacks and a first aid kit. It is also good practice to have participants sign a liability waiver prior to embarking on the hiking event.

ICE CREAM SOCIAL

"I scream, you scream...we all scream for ice cream!" Who doesn't love an ice cream social? In an era where we are so often glued to our computers, an ice cream social is the perfect way to bring community members together and support a great cause.

Sell each dish or cone of ice cream for a set amount.

How do you get the ice cream to your event? There are many options; below are a few to consider:

*Ask a local vendor to borrow a machine in exchange for advertising.
*Make the ice cream yourself. Find serving tables that freeze or a freezer that you can utilize.
*Work with a local ice cream shop. Ask that they donate a set percentage of funds from a specific day (and set hours) of sales.

Don't forget to bring toppings! Sprinkles, nuts…and more.

Remember to provide plenty of seating. Whether your event is indoors or outdoors, seating is a must. If people stay, they are more likely to buy more ice cream and/or participate in your add-on events.

As an add-on to this event, you can raise additional funds by including a 50/50 raffle, a reverse raffle and/or face painting. Consider hosting your event outdoors at a local park.

RAKE IT UP!

Grab your rakes! Designate volunteers in various neighborhoods to rake leaves from yards in exchange for a donation to your organization. Arm volunteers with flyers for your group. You can spread the word in advance or you can simply go door-to-door when the leaves begin to fall, and explain that you are raking leaves for a good cause. Depending on the amount of volunteers participating, your organization can raise $500 or more.

Request a $20 donation for each yard raked (you may need to charge more for very large yards). If you have 5 sets of volunteers who each rake just 5 yards in one week, you will bring in $500 for your cause (and you'll get a great workout while enjoying the fresh air)!

SCRAPBOOK A-THON

Whether you love to scrapbook or you're new to the scene, hosting a scrapbook-a-thon is a lot fun! Set a location, date and time for your event. Charge an entry fee to attend. Ask attendees to BYOS *(bring your own supplies)* and encourage everyone to share and swap supplies with each other. You can host a scrapbook-a-thon in a volunteer's home, if they have a large enough space (including a lot of table space). Offer free refreshments and pizza to attendees. Ask others to bring old scrapbooks to share (providing new ideas to other attendees). Play a movie or music during the event. Have plenty of table space available, as well as extra tape, scissors and glue.

Raffle a spa-themed basket (or a scrapbook basket) to add additional excitement (and raise additional funds). You may also consider adding a 50/50 raffle to your event.

CRAZY HAT DAY

Hold this fundraiser once a year or once a month - you decide! Collaborate with your school district to host a CRAZY HAT DAY. Students pay $1.00 (or any amount you have determined appropriate) on CRAZY HAT DAY and they can wear their crazy hats to school. Each classroom teacher collects the funds for his/her students.

You may consider offering a "pre-sale" and allowing parents and teachers to donate to the CRAZY HAT fund. If a teacher donates $2 to the fund, he/she will be given two-free CRAZY HAT passes (one for each dollar donated). The teacher then uses their free pass as a reward for a well-behaved student.

To take this fundraiser a step further, consider hosting a CRAZY HAT contest during lunch period (i.e. most creative hat) and offer small prizes for the winners in each category.

TRIVIA NIGHT

If you enjoy competition - trivia night is a great way to raise funds for your cause! Collect an entry fee of $10 per person and provide prizes to the top three individuals or teams (depending on how you structure the event). HINT: Use donated items as prizes (i.e. restaurant gift cards, spa package). Set the date, time and location of your event. Provide a list of prizes and a rule sheet prior to the event.

To raise attendance, you may consider offering a pre-sale (i.e. tickets purchased one week prior to the event are just $8/each) *and* offer ticket sales that night for $10-12/each.

Choose a theme for your Trivia Night fundraiser event (i.e. movies, books, music).

Consider hosting this event on a regular basis. Holding the event once a month will draw a larger crowd and additional funds for your cause (you can choose a different theme for each month).

You can also raise additional funds by offering a 50/50 raffle at your event.

BENCH-A-THON

Participants collect pledges for every pound they lift. Individuals then bench press weights on a set date and time.

A school weight room or a YMCA is a great place to hold this event. Be sure to have all participants sign a liability waiver. It is crucial that all participants have a proper spotter during lifting, too.

Be sure to have participants sign a liability waiver prior to participation in the event. Having medical professionals at the event is highly recommended.

TIP: You can host a similar fundraiser for your group doing push-ups (no equipment or spotters required). Push-ups allow you to host your fundraiser event indoors or outdoors.

PAY IT FORWARD

Gather a group of volunteers or supporters in your organization. Give each individual $10. Set a specific amount of time (i.e. three-hours) to use the funds, raising as much as each person can for the cause.

This fundraiser requires thinking outside of the box. Creativity is the name of the game. It's a great way to get out in your local community and spread the word about the work your organization is doing. It is also a great way to raise funds. You never know what new ideas your volunteers will develop. Who knows, you may stumble upon a catchy fundraiser idea that turns into an annual event!

MAKE THE GRADE

Hold this fundraiser quarterly throughout the school year. Ask students to request pledges for the number of A's and B's they earn on their report card. Students are given a pledge sheet at the start of each quarter. At the end of the quarter, when grades are released, they follow up with sponsors to collect pledges. This is a great way to support a local cause and motivate students to work toward good grades!

IT'S A BUST!

Sell balloons for $5 – 10/each. When a supporter buys a balloon - give them a raffle ticket (not the balloon).

Prior to the fundraiser, insert a number into each balloon. The number should correspond to a raffle ticket given to the purchaser. Be sure to keep a well-organized list.

Let everyone know what time you will pop the balloons (announce prizes). Pop a balloon for each available prize and announce the winning number. (Attempt to have prizes donated from local businesses prior to your event). Winners must be present to win their prize.

STAY AT HOME EVENT

It might sound silly, but it works! Mail out invitations to a "made-up" event and offer invitees tickets to support your cause. You can call the event "Cozy at Home" or another creative name. The perk is - no one has to leave home!

This is a creative way to request donations for your organization. Be sure to create professional invites and include a self-addressed, pre-stamped envelope to your organization (make it as easy as possible to donate!). It is also important to include your website address, inviting everyone to donate online, if they prefer.

NOTE: This fundraiser works best once your organization has built long-standing trust and credibility within your community. Community (invitees) need to know how your organization is helping the community (and see you in action).

TEXT FOR A CAUSE

Utilize a service that allows your organization to receive donations of $5-10 from text messages. *Mobile Giving* is one of many services that work with non-profit organizations.

Choose a service for your organization to work with for this fundraiser. Determine a specific word or phrase that you wish to have supporter's text to donate.

TIP: Please remind your supporters to not text and drive!

Find more information on Mobile Giving: *www.mobilegiving.org*

SCRATCH CARDS

Sell scratch cards to your supporters during a one week (or one month) fundraising campaign. You can also sell scratch cards during another event for your organization.

Scratch cards can have three scratch-off areas. Have designated prizes ready in advance and tailor your scratch card winnings to fit those prizes. This works best when you have a variety of small prizes and a few big prizes.

The more tickets you sell, the more funds you raise for your cause!

How to create your own scratch cards

SUPPLY LIST
Cardboard
A print-out of your lottery ticket
Glue stick
Sticky back plastic (contact paper)
Metallic Acrylic paint (silver)
Washing Liquid

STEPS
1. Print out the design that you want to show on your lottery ticket (thick paper is preferred)
2. Use a piece of sticky back plastic and place on top of your printed design
3. Mix a dash of metallic paint with washing liquid (works best if mixed on a paper plate).

Recommended mix: 1 part washing liquid to 2 parts paint. Mix.

4. With your plastic piece in place, on top of your printed design: paint the plastic with your mix from Step 3 (make sure that the picture under the paint is hidden. You may need to add a second layer of paint). Let dry.

5. You're done! Now your ticket is ready to be sold and scratched!

BONUS IDEA: You can also supply donors with a sheet of coupons for a small donation.

IT TASTES SO SWEET

Ask the local high school if your organization can set up a baked goods table at a basketball game or other popular event.

Ask supporters to donate baked goods and set up your table. Clearly mark the price of each item with a price tag, or consider selling all items for the same amount (i.e. $1 for each item or buy 10 items for just $8!).

Be sure to stay for the entire event, if possible. Items will sell best at the start of the event, half-time and at the end.

BIG MONEY MAKING IDEAS

SILENT AUCTION/DINNER

Hosting an annual silent auction/dinner fundraiser is a great way to gather your supporters together and raise funds for a great cause! Silent auction events are exciting and can be as formal or informal as you desire. Just remember to choose the appropriate location and ticket price for your event.

Suggested steps to planning a silent auction/dinner fundraiser:

1) Nine to twelve months prior to your event, secure the location, date and time. Be sure your event is easy to find and offers ample parking.
2) Interview (taste test) local caterers and decide your menu. Will your caterers supply servers? Dinnerware? Drinks? Tablecloths/linens?
3) Will you offer alcohol at your event? Will it be sold through the venue or do you need to hire a separate bartender?
4) Purchase insurance for your event.
5) Designate a volunteer committee for silent auction items. The committee should begin soliciting donated items approximately nine months in advance, and continue until two weeks prior to the event.
6) Designate a volunteer committee for the décor of your event. Set a budget (i.e. balloons, flowers).
7) Designate a volunteer committee to secure corporate sponsors for your event.

8) Communication is essential! As the event coordinator, check-in with each volunteer and each committee no less than once a month (nine months leading up to the event). As the event nears, you will want to meet/check-in with more frequency.

9) Where will you safely hold donated items throughout the year? Designate a large, temperature controlled, safe place for donated items.

10) Who is in charge of tracking expenses? Keep an organized spreadsheet.

11) Who is in charge of tracking secured corporate sponsors? What will your corporate sponsors receive in return for their support?

12) Who is in charge of tracking collected donations/items for the silent auction? How will you share information on newly donated items, with your volunteers/employees and supporters?

13) Will you be hiring a live musician? An emcee?

14) What is your donation goal? Keep a close eye on expenses. You can spend a lot while setting up a great event. Remember, the goal is to *raise* funds!

15) Set your ticket price. What does a ticket include?

16) Create professional event programs for every guest.

17) Create professional signs for your event (i.e. silent auction rule sheet, open and closing bidding times).

18) As the event nears, plan your advertising strategy. Are you able to advertise on the radio? Local news stations? Press release? Who will design your invitations and when and who will you mail invites to?

19) Plan a date and time to gather volunteers together, to put together baskets. You will need to put together themed baskets several days before the event (additional items always arrive last-minute). Create a minimum bid amount (starting bid) for each themed basket (i.e. Spa Basket – starting bid $40). NOTE: It is crucial that you document every basket. Assign a number or letter(s) to every basket and keep a list of every item included in that basket, the starting bid, and the estimated value.

20) Create professional bid sheets. Place a bid sheet with each basket. Bid sheets should list every item included in the basket.

21) Raise awareness, sell tickets! Spread the word, send invites and keep careful track of ticket sales. Assign every ticket purchaser a silent auction bidding number. *Keep an organized list!* Mail tickets and include directions and a phone number to your event.

The day of your event:

1) Arrive early! Stay calm. Rely on your organization. There will be stressful moments today; expect them upfront and realize that every issue that arises is "figure-outable". You've spent nine to twelve months carefully planning and organizing your event. Attendees are thrilled to support your organization. Take a deep breath, stay focused and get ready for the fun to begin!

2) In the morning, confirm catering. Confirm delivery of your completed silent auction baskets. Arrange the décor. Arrange the seating. Arrange silent auction tables and linens. Set up your welcome/sign-in table.

3) Make sure the inside and outside of venue are professional and ready to go!

4) Set up directional signs to your event (arrows pointing to parking).

5) Schedule volunteers to arrive early to help with preparations.

6) Offer a small thank you gift to volunteers who have worked hard on the event.

7) An hour before the event be sure everything is ready to go. Staff the welcome table. As each attendee arrives, mark names off the check-in list and provide each attendee with a physical silent auction number. Explain what time bidding opens and when dinner is served. Inform guests of any specific seating arrangements or additional activities offered.

8) Don't forget to have fun! Mingle. Thank everyone for coming to support your organization. Enjoy the food, music, silent auction items – all while raising funds for a great local cause!

Optional Add-On Ideas:

*You may add additional fundraiser activities to your event, such as: 50/50 raffle, motivational speaker, live music/band.
*Will your CEO, Executive Director or Group Leader offer a short speech during the event?
*Consider grouping like items together for bidding (i.e. event ticket items, sport-themed items, art).
*Do have the number to a taxi service available, if needed.
*Hire a photographer for your event
*Designate a V.I.P. table(s)/section
*Offer a professionally created (silent) slide show. Show the slide show on repeat at one end of the room.

WINE TASTING

Host a wine tasting fundraiser for your organization! Wine tasting fundraisers work well when held as annual fundraisers. If you're considering hosting your first wine tasting fundraiser, work with a local winery or restaurant to plan your event. When working with a local venue you will have the knowledge and expertise of those who have been in the wine industry for years. In addition, you will have an elegant atmosphere for your event!

After securing a winery to work with and scheduling your event's date and time, below are a few helpful tips and reminders when planning your event:

*Sign a contract, stating the percentage of proceeds your organization will receive.
*Does the winery require a minimum number of attendees?
*Know exactly what the winery will provide for your attendees (i.e. what type of wine, how much, length of explanation, any food/appetizers?).
*Discuss with the winery, will their insurance cover the event, or do you need to purchase your own insurance?
*Is there a maximum number of attendees for your location/event?
*Design professional invitations for your fundraiser event. Set your ticket price. Remember, you are hosting the event to *raise* funds for your organization!
*Promote your event. Consider a creative name for your event (i.e. Wine & Dine for _____).

*Will you offer a gift to attendees (i.e. custom wine bag with your organization's logo)?

CONCERT

Who doesn't love good music? You can host a battle of the bands (working with local bands/groups) or a one-band concert - you decide. Either host the concert indoors at a rented venue or space or host the concert outdoors at a park. There are a lot of options when it comes to this fundraising event!

You can hire a band or find bands/musician(s) to volunteer their time and efforts for the event.

Determine the ticket price by the number of bands playing, the location/venue for your event and if you offer food and or/refreshments with the cost of the ticket. Selling food and refreshments separately at your event can greatly boost the amount of funds raised.

As with all events – large or small - promotion is important! Spread the word with flyers, social media posts, blog posts, a press release, local news appearance…any creative outlet you can think of.

5K RUN/WALK

Creating and hosting an annual 5K run/walk event for your organization is a great way to raise funds and bring the community together. As with any large event, there is a lot of planning and preparation involved - but the end result is worth it! Begin planning your event a minimum of nine months in advance.

Must do's:

*Create an online registration form (make sure registration is quick and easy!)
*Determine the 5K location. Where do most of your supporters live? Are hotels available for out-of-town runners/walkers?
*Create your race course. Will your course be out and back or a loop? (Choose one of these options to avoid transporting walkers/runners).
*Determine your entry fee. What is the pre-registration fee? What do participants get for their entry fee? (i.e. race bag)
*Is your course through a park? On a trail? On a bike path? Sidewalks? Roadways? Do you need assistance with blocking traffic? Have you spoken with your local police department?
*Do you have a race clock (showing running times)?
*Work to gather donated Gatorade, water, bananas and other items for participants.
*What will distinguish your finish line?
*What will indicate your start line? Who will officially announce the start of the race?

*Will you have chip timers available for participants? Will participants wear bib/race numbers?

*Collect donated prizes for race winners. Decide ahead of time how many prizes you will award and for what categories (i.e. overall male and female winners, age group winners).

*Create a professional map of the race course to provide to participants.

*Gather a large group of volunteers for the event day. Volunteers should wear matching attire. Volunteers will assist with starting the race, directional support during the race, aid stations, finish line organization and clean-up.

*Are restrooms available? Do you need to rent Port-a-Potty's?

*Will you provide a finishers ribbon or medal to every participant?

*Where will you place trash cans for participants and spectators to utilize?

*Plan ahead to have plenty of: tables, chairs, tents, cups, refreshments, coolers, ribbons/finishers awards--- and volunteers!

Additional considerations:

- Sell race shirts or other apparel to raise additional funds for your cause.
- Sell wristbands/bracelets for your organization to raise additional funds at the race.
- Offer a 50/50 raffle. Participants and spectators can enter to win.

- Create a theme for your 5K event (i.e. center it around Halloween, for example).
- Invite a local band(s) to play during the 5K run/walk event.
- Will a local business sponsor your event?
- Be sure to check with your local government to determine what permits the race requires. Most likely insurance coverage for your event is required.
- Safety and security are crucial elements of your event. Make sure to have proper traffic safety devices (i.e. cones, crowd control barricades), et cetera.
- Arrange to have medical professionals on hand, in case of an emergency (i.e. EMT's and/or a tent in the finish area with doctors and nurses on hand to help with minor medical issues).
- Many race events offer a free five-minute massage tent/area at the finish area.
- Have plenty of safety pins (for bib numbers) available!
- It's a nice touch to invite a photographer(s) to the event to capture photos of participants during the race and at the finish line. You can sell "finishers photos" online after the event, to raise additional funds for your cause.
- Don't forget to post the race results prior to the awards ceremony. It is also good practice to post the race results on your website following the event.
- Host a "fun run" event, following the 5K run/walk. Fun Run's are generally 200-400 meters in distance and are open to children under age 10 or 11. Fun Run's are free and are a great way to add extra pizzazz to your event.

- Add a face painting booth/area to raise additional funds for your cause.

ART SHOW

Art shows are a great way to raise funds for your charity. First, decide if your event will be an art show or an art sale. Once you have decided the premise of your event, along with the venue, date and time - you're ready to get to work. Begin planning your art show or art sale event at least nine months in advance.

Points to remember:

*If you are hosting an art sale, hire an experienced art auctioneer. The auctioneer needs to know art so that they can properly explain each piece to potential buyers.
*How will you display art pieces?
*Provide a brief artist bio and description of the piece for every art work.
*Send professionally designed invitations prior to the event.
*Set a ticket price. What will attendees get for the cost of their ticket? (i.e. refreshments included?)
*Consider adding corporate sponsors to your event.
*Raffle a specific art item of art to add extra excitement to your event.
*Be aware of the maximum number of attendees your venue can hold.
*Will buyers be responsible for taking home purchased items that evening or will they need to arrange a delivery or pick-up at a later time?
*Hire a local musician for background music at the event.

*Consider hiring a professional photographer for the event.

T-SHIRT SALE

Work with a local print shop to design and print shirts for your organization. Use your logo and a catchy phrase or line (i.e. *"Keep Calm and _____".* Fill in the blank with anything that works for your cause. For example, if you are a cat rescue, you can create shirts that say *"Keep Calm and Love a Cat").*

Discuss your fundraising goal with the local print shop. How many shirts do you need to order to obtain the best deal/price? What price do you need to sell each shirt in order to make a profit for your cause?

Next, decide where and how you will sell your apparel. Will you sell them online (via social media and your website) or at an event?

T-shirt sales require a slight risk due to upfront costs. However, if you have a solid sales plan in place (and an eye-catching shirt!), you can raise significant funds for your organization with this fundraiser.

SCAVENGER HUNT

If you love playing games and being outdoors, a scavenger hunt is a great way to raise funds for your cause! Hosting the scavenger hunt as an annual event will allow you to grow the fundraiser each year.

Charge a set registration fee for participants. Will you require registration as an individual? As teams? Both? Will participants receive a t-shirt as part of their entry fee?

What will you hide for your scavenger hunt? Be sure that hidden items are not too valuable (in the event that they become lost or ruined).

Be sure the scavenger hunt is challenging, but not so difficult that it discourages participants from continuing their journey. The event should be fun!

How does it work?

*Consider creating a theme for your event (i.e. *Winter Scavenger Hunt*. Everything on the scavenger hunt list could be winter related, such as: a blue candy cane, a specific ornament).
*At the start of the event, provide individuals/teams with the list of items they need to find. Provide a map of the area where all items are found (i.e. inside of one specific large building, one street, one neighborhood).
*Set a time limit. A shorter time period will make the event more exciting. Try to keep the list of items

under 25 and the time limit to no more than two-hours. Whoever finds the most items on the list, in the designated amount of time, wins.

*Collect donated awards prior to the event. Award the top three individuals/teams (i.e. gift cards).

*Provide refreshments (try to have items donated for your event).

*Keep safety in mind! How will you keep your event and attendees safe? Plan ahead. If your event is outdoors, what will you do in the case of inclement weather?

BIKE RELAY

Hosting a bike relay fundraiser is similar to hosting a 5K run/walk, in terms of preparation. However, there are additional elements to consider with a bike relay.

*Determine the bike relay course. What is the total distance? How many miles with each participant pedal? Will your overall course be out and back or a loop?
*Determine your entry fee.
*Bike relays often cover a lot of distance. If your event crosses into various towns and counties, be sure to check with every municipality regarding permits, regulations, safety and insurance.
*Insurance is a must.
*Liability waivers are a must.
*Establish a group of volunteers at: the start of the race, at each location/station where a participant finishes and a new relay participant begins, and at the finish.
*Will you provide transportation for bikers?
*Create a professional course map to provide to participants and interested spectators and supporters.
*Require all participants to wear a helmet.
*Establish several aid stations throughout your course and obtain volunteers to man the aid stations.
*Have medical professionals on hand in case of emergency (i.e. doctors, nurses).
*Consider finding event sponsorship from local businesses.
*Plan an awards ceremony following the event. Will you provide a winner's medal or ribbon to every

finisher? What awards will you provide to the top three teams (i.e. Cash, gift cards)?

*Do you have an official timer for the event? How will you document the splits of each relay participant (i.e. are cyclist wearing timing chips)?

*Provide restrooms or Port-a-Potties at the start/finish and at each relay exchange area.

*Offer easy online registration.

*How will you provide safety during your event? Speak with your local police department.

DANCE MARATHON

Hire a D.J., select a venue and dance the night away for a good cause! When hosting a dance marathon fundraiser event for the first time, set a goal of 100 attendees. Each participant pays a fee to enter. Participants can also gain pledges for every hour they continue dancing. Gain 100 attendees, each raising $100 (including their entry fee), and you will have raised $10,000 for your cause (minus your expenses).

What to know:

*Select a large, elegant venue.
*Hire a D.J.
*Provide refreshments and snacks.
*Hire a photographer.
*Accept online registration and pledges (make it easy to donate)!
*Assign each dancer/participant a number.
*Provide prizes to the top three dancers (those who dance the longest).
*Remember, the more dancers/participants you have, the more funds you will raise.
*Plan to have volunteers assisting with coat check, welcoming (providing dance numbers/sign-in), monitoring dancers, refreshments, et cetera.
*Establish a volunteer decorating committee for the event.
*Consider a theme for your event.
*Hosting the dance marathon as an annual event will help draw a larger crowd each year.

*Hosting a large-scale event on a small budget is a big challenge - but it's possible! Keep track of your expenses and remember, you are hosting the event to *raise* funds for your cause!

FASHION SHOW

You will need to gather a significant number of volunteers for this event. A fashion show is an exciting and fun event when well-planned. Begin planning a minimum of nine months in advance. Consider collaborating with your local mall to help draw a larger crowd. Once you have established your venue, date and location – the real work begins.

Appoint a volunteer committee for decorating the event. Appoint another committee to find volunteer clothing models. Establish a third committee for seeking corporate event sponsors and obtaining donated raffle items for the fashion show event (a raffle provides an additional source of raising funds). Appoint a fourth committee to find support people (i.e. volunteer hairstylists, make-up artists, music coordinators).

Decide if you would like to work with local stores (to borrow or purchase clothes to model) or if you would like your models to purchase clothes from particular stores, to model.

What is the theme of your fashion show? Decide on a theme and be sure that the clothes being modeled reflect that theme.

Create professional invitations and flyers. Begin spreading the word (and selling tickets to the event).

Schedule a photographer for your event (do you have a volunteer or board member who can fill this role?).

Create a website page and sell tickets directly from your website (as well as in-person). Make it quick and easy to purchase a ticket to the big event.

Determine the length of your event. What will attendees get for the price of their admission ticket (i.e. a goodie bag with donated sample items such as perfume)?

BACHELOR/BACHELOETTE AUCTION

A matchmaker fundraiser is a unique way to raise awareness and funds for your organization. Whether you're an animal welfare organization or a food bank, hosting a matchmaker auction can be a highly successful fundraiser for your cause. And who knows, you may bring two people together who would have otherwise never met!

What do you need for a successful matchmaker event?

Prior to the event, speak with local businesses (i.e. restaurants, bars, theaters). Ask for donated gift certificates. Utilize the donated certificates to create gift packages for matches made at the auction.

*Find a location with a stage (having a stage makes it easier to see who you are bidding on).
*Hire an emcee for your event.
*Consider asking a photographer to volunteer for your event, or hire a photographer.
*Decide *who* will be auctioned. Do you know singles who would like to support your organization/cause and participate in your event? Never guilt or force someone to participate in the auction - there are always other volunteer opportunities!
*Consider inviting a local single celebrity (i.e. local band member, local radio or television personality).
*Design a color hand-out for every guest. The hand-out should include a headshot and brief bio of every

participant in the auction. (Hint: Include an interesting fact or favorite quote from each person). *You can operate your event with live bidding (shouting the bids) or in silent auction style (write bids on a sheet next to the potential dates color photo and bio).

When a match is created, present the couple with a donated gift package (allow the match to decide when they will utilize the gift certificates).

It is helpful to create several volunteer committees to help with the event (i.e. decorating, soliciting donations). Don't forget to have fun! This event can draw a large crowd, translating into significant donations for your cause.

GOLF TOURNAMENT

Golf tournaments are very lucrative for non-profit organizations and causes. Begin planning your event a minimum of six months in advance. When determining a date and location for your event, be sure to check the calendar. Will other large golf tournaments be hosted in your area at that time? Choosing the best date for your event is essential to success.

When selecting your volunteer planning committee for the golf tournament, include a variety of individuals (i.e. those experienced with golf, others experienced with coordinating fundraising events).

"A critical step in the planning process is the selection of the actual golf course. To gain instant credibility with the golf community, sponsors and guest pros who attend, choose an exclusive course that is highly rated in your area. Try to avoid a local community course just because it fits within your schedule or budget. If it is a "members only" course, find out who is on their board and determine if you have any contacts to reach out to these members to obtain approval for your organization to use the course. Be sure to consider the costs that some of these more elite courses may charge, and if there are high fees, consider asking a local business to pick up this tab by being "title" sponsor of your charity golf outing." Explains *Golf Registrations*.

Do you know your total costs? Are you required to have a minimum number of golfers? Break it down: cost per golfer; food and refreshment cost.

Create an agreement prior to the event, signed by all involved parties. Be sure to include the cancellation terms and weather policy, as well as a detailed description of tournament services (i.e. golf carts, gratuities, et cetera).

Don't forget the goody bags! Create a thank you bag for every participant. Include items such as: tees, golf balls, small promotional items and/or gift certificates from corporate sponsors.

Additional considerations:

*Designate who (a committee or group of people) will solicit corporate sponsorships and donations for the event.
*Who will design the logo and webpage for your golf tournament?
*How will you market/advertise your event?
*Will you hire a photographer?
*Who will supply tents? Refreshments? Food?
*Have you designated a welcome committee (i.e. registration, goody bag distribution, welcoming attendees)?
*Will you offer a raffle? This is a great way to raise additional funds for your cause.
*Do you have a Judging Panel in place? Locate several volunteers to judge on-course contests and to help keep general order on the course during your

event (make sure volunteers in this position are knowledgeable and experienced golfers).

Don't forget to offer online pre-registration for your event. Registration should be quick and easy. The higher your attendance, the more funds you can raise for your cause!

EATING CONTEST

Ready! Set! Eat!

Who doesn't love a good eating contest? Select the food and let the fun begin! Whether your food of choice is doughnuts or cookies, eating contests can raise ample funds for your cause. Draw a crowd and let the magic begin.

There are two ways to operate an eating contest for your organization:

1) Designate a certain amount of food for each contestant. Whoever eats their food the fastest, wins.
2) Designate a set amount of time. Whoever eats the most food in that amount of time, wins.

Participants pay an entry fee. Spectators can pay a small fee as well. All fees go to your organization (be sure to factor in the cost of food, location rental, et cetera).

Provide a shirt or bib to every contestant, with your organization name and logo.

Prior to the event, solicit donations from local businesses for your event prize packages (i.e. gift certificates, event tickets).

Invite your local television news or radio station to cover the event; this helps raise additional funds and awareness for your organization.

BOOK FAIR

Collect gently used books for your big event. Select a date and location for your event. Consider working with a large local bookstore or your local library. Can you host your event under a large tent in front of their facility? In addition, consider hosting the event for a full weekend (Saturday and Sunday) to gain additional sales and exposure for your cause.

Arrange books into categories (i.e. mystery, self-help) and clearly label. Remember, the more books you have to sell, the more funds you can raise for your organization.

Add a 50/50 raffle to your event for extra pizzazz (and to help draw a larger crowd). Playing music during your event can also provide a positive boost to the atmosphere, and often can assist in generating additional sales.

Be sure a donation jar and an information table with your organization's information, flyers, et cetera is available . Hosting the event annually will boost attendance numbers, too. Begin collecting books one-year prior to your event.

BONUS: As we have entered into a digital age of reading (i.e. Kindle, Nook), create a catchy sign to draw people to your event. One bookstore created an interesting sign that worked wonders for their business. It simply said:

REAL BOOKS NEVER DIE

And they drew a simple sketch of a battery on low.

Source: Pinterest

CHILDREN'S ART EXHIBIT

Determine your event location and date one year in advance and let the fun begin! Collect children's art work throughout the year. Place paintings and drawings in frames. Other works of art are encouraged, as well (i.e. quilts).

If your organization utilizes social media, it is a good idea to post a photo of each piece of donated work, to thank the donor and to encourage others to donate items to your fundraiser, too.

Provide a free pass for every child who donates art work (along with one free adult pass).

Raise funds by charging an admission fee for attendees the night of your event. Also, sell the donated art work to raise funds. (As always, you can raise additional funds by adding a raffle, selling shirts). Admission should include light refreshments (and possibly food).

This is a great event to bring everyone in the community together for a worthy cause.

CHOCOLATE TASTE FEST

Who doesn't love chocolate? Hosting a chocolate taste fest is a sure way to grab the attention of your supporters and community members. Consider hosting your event annually. Host the event at a local park or a rented venue, depending on the time of year and anticipated size of the crowd.

A few things to remember:

*Solicit corporate sponsorships for your event (begin a minimum of six months prior to your event).
*Who will supply your chocolate? Work with local vendors and businesses to offer a variety of chocolate options. Charge a booth rental fee for businesses to attend. Require that every booth offer a food sample (i.e. must be chocolate).
*Charge an admission fee to your event (i.e. $5 per person, children under age 8 are free). The bulk of your funds are raised through booth rentals.
*Invite local television and radio stations to attend your event,
*Spread the word. Write a press release, hang flyers around your community, utilize social media, ask participating businesses to hang event flyers in their store windows.

COMEDY NIGHT

Who doesn't love to laugh? Laughter provides many benefits, too.

Laughter…

*Improves alertness, creativity and memory.
*Lowers blood pressure.
*Humor during class/course instruction has been proven to lead to increased test scores.
*Defends against respiratory infections (laughter can even reduce the frequency of colds)!
*Reduces certain stress hormones (i.e. cortisol, adrenaline).
*Increases vascular blood flow and oxygenation of the blood.

Knowing the many benefits of laughter, why not laugh for a good cause?

Collect an admission fee for your comedy night fundraiser. You can also sell refreshments and food, and offer a raffle (of baskets, specific items or a 50/50 raffle) to raise additional funds.

Ask local comedians and others to volunteer their time for the event.

Consider hosting a comedy night on a regular basis, to benefit your charity or cause. Remember, the larger the crowd you can draw, the more funds you can raise!

NOTE: You can also host a comedy contest. Ask attendees to vote on the best comedian and provide a prize.

HALLOWEEN DRESS-UP CONTEST

A Halloween-themed party can work for any age group. You can host a family friendly event and provide prizes for each age group winner. Consider utilizing a venue that offers a stage for guests to model their Halloween costumes.

The cost of the admission ticket should include optional participation in the costume contest, food and refreshments. Jazz up your event by providing an emcee and/or a local musician. Locate a volunteer photographer to capture fun moments from your event.

Consider adding additional money makers to your event such as raffles, shirt-sales, et cetera.

DUCKIE RACE

A duck (or "duckie) race involves yellow plastic ducks. *A lot of them!* Participants purchase a duck. Every duck has a number. On the day of the event, dump all of the ducks into a body of water and the duck who floats across the finish line first, is the winner.

Duckie races can raise significant funds for your organization. As with most large fundraisers, begin planning your event at least six months in advance.

Important points to remember as you plan:

*Large bags of "racing ducks" can be ordered from fundraising supply companies. You also have the option to rent ducks from various companies (or you may consider asking another large organization in your area if you can rent or borrow their racing ducks).

*Label each racing duck with a *waterproof* marker (very important!)

*Keep organized records (know which number corresponds with which individual).

*Decide ahead of time if the winner must be present to win. If not, be sure to collect phone numbers when tickets (ducks) are purchased.

*How many prizes will you offer? Work on collecting donated prize items prior to the event. Remember, the prizes you offer can draw a larger crowd!

*Decide on ticket costs (per duckie).

*Add an additional money-maker on your event day. For example, host a "GUESS THE TIME" event. Keep an oversized chart of possible finishing times for the winning duckie. People pay $5 to place their name next to a time guess. Provide a prize to the winner with the closest guess.

*Additional events to consider offering on your event day (to raise additional funds):
   - Face painting
   - Raffle items
   - Silent Auction items
   - Games/competitions
   - Sell refreshments/food

NOTE: As an alternative to the duckie race, consider hosting a message in a bottle race. Use plastic bottles and place a note inside of each bottle with the name of the ticket purchaser. Utilize the same concept: the bottle that crosses the finish line first, is the winner.

REMINDERS: Be certain to gain approval for waterway use prior to your event!

Block off a controlled area of water for your event (to allow for easy clean-up). Exercise proper clean-up procedures following your fundraiser event. Keep waterways clean and free of debris. It is a good policy to leave the waterway cleaner than when you first arrived.

FAMILY PORTRAIT NIGHT

A family portrait night invites everyone in the community to come out and have a professional photograph taken with their loved ones. Portraits can include children, couples, grandparents, people and their pets, et cetera.

Decide where you will host the event. Will the event be outdoors? At a park? A rented indoor venue?

Work with local professional photographers. Will they volunteer their time and talents to help your cause?

Once the location is established and photographers confirmed, you're on your way! Decide on a portrait price and get to work on the details. Will attendees be able to view an immediate digital version of the photograph? Will the final photograph be e-mailed to attendees or will prints be made and ready for pick-up? What will your photographers utilize as a background for portraits?

Adding additional money makers to your event will increase excitement (and funds raised).

OPEN HOUSE EVENT

An open house event is a fun way to invite community members to visit your facility, get to know your volunteers and employees and donate to a great cause. Offer your open house as a free event, open to the public. Sell refreshments and food to raise funds. You can also sell apparel with your organizations logo, to raise additional funds.

As another variation of this event, consider hosting an open house event that requires ticket sales. A purchased ticket includes an evening of wine and appetizers as well as mingling and meeting your organizations staff and volunteers.

Many people think Open House events are for "Grand Openings"- but that's not true! Consider hosting an annual Open House event to raise awareness and funds for your organization. Designate a volunteer committee to help with décor, wine/refreshments, et cetera. It is important to appoint several volunteers to provide tours of your facility to interested guests.

BONUS TIPS:

*Offer a slide-show (played on repeat) on an empty wall. Make sure the slideshow is silent and shows various photographs of the work your organization performs in the community.
*Mail invitations to local businesses ("Get to know your neighbors") and other non-profit organizations in the community.

*Locate a local musician to play background music during the event.
*Provide a gift bag or a logo item for guests to take home from the event (i.e. bumper sticker, key chain).

IMPROV NIGHT

Come one, come all to Improv Night! Charge an admission fee and let the fun begin. Improv Night is sure to bring a lot of laughs. This fundraiser will bring the community together, all while raising funds for a great cause. Charge an admission fee to raise funds.

Don't forget to include the audience in the improv act! How do you do that? Play games! One such game is called "Bus Stop". The actors act like they are driving a bus and go out into the audience to collect bus riders. The rest…is up to you. This is improv, after all.

This fundraiser works best at a venue with a stage. Consider collaborating with your local high school to utilize a large, functional space – and if possible, improv actors.

There are no limits to the cues and games played during improv night. A few additional suggestions (to get you started), include:

*"Dinner Party." Your actors are hosting a dinner party and need to invite four guests (from the audience) to attend. Assign silly jobs or names to the invited guests (i.e. body builder, Pee Wee Herman).

*Sing-A-Long. Actors and their "invited" (audience) guests can only sing their lines.

Pick a topic. Have a bucket full of random topic ideas for improv night. An audience member pulls a topic and announces it to the actors.

MOTIVATIONAL SPEAKER

Hire a motivational speaker and invite attendees to raise funds for your cause. Be sure to know your expenses up front, so you can determine your ticket price and know how many tickets you need to sell to make a profit for your cause.

A motivational speaker can be a sports figure, a local university sports coach, a musician, an author or a professor. You may also consider collecting a group of motivational speakers for your event. Why not ask each speaker to talk for a set amount of time. Attendees will gain knowledge and stories from multiple speakers.

Sell items with your organization's logo (during and after the event). Have a booth set up for this purpose near the entrance/exit.

Motivational speakers can:

*Increase self-confidence/esteem
*Bring people together
*Inspire creativity and entrepreneurship
*Inspire individuality
*Motivate community members to stand behind a great cause (i.e. your organization!)

Consider collaborating with your local high school or university to utilize a gymnasium for the event. You will need ample seating and parking for your guests.

POKER TOURNAMENT

Set the rules for your event. Which type of poker will be played (i.e. Texas Hold'em)? What is the buy-in? What will the prize pot be worth?

What you will need:

- Location
- Tables
- Chairs
- Experienced Poker players
- Several decks of cards
- Several sets of chips
- Volunteer "Dealers"

WikiHow explains, "**Once everybody has registered and submitted their buy-in money, divide people up into groups.** This will depend on how many people you have, but separating people into tables of six to ten players will work. Do not lock the tourney line-up in advance of game day; take seat reservations in advance, but a tourney will see a lot of walk up players on game day if it is well-publicized."

Everyone should begin with the same number of chips at the start of the tournament.

As the tournament continues, eventually there will only be one table left with the best players. Continue the game until you have a clear winner. The money goes to the winner. Decide in advance, will the winner's money be split 50/50 with the charity organization? Be clear on the rules prior to starting your event.

TIPS TO REMEMBER:

*Stay organized and keep careful records. Who will be in charge of the money? What checks and balances do you have in place for the event?
*Check your local laws to ensure your fundraiser is legal – and following all of the proper rules.
*Check with your insurance agent. What insurance will you need to have in place for this event?
*Consider collaborating with a local poker hall. Charity poker halls can help you get your license and ensure legal compliance. Often, they will provide dealers and run the games. When working with a charity poker hall, you will do less work and have greater potential for your event.

BINGO NIGHT

B-I-N-G-O, B-I-N-G-O, B-I-N-G-O and Bingo was his name-o!

Select a large open space for your event. Consider utilizing a local high school gymnasium or cafeteria for your event.

What you need:

*Bingo Callers (experienced bingo callers can help your event run smoothly)!
*Bingo books (and additional bingo sheets for jackpot games)
*Bingo daubers (markers for the players)
*Tables and chairs for attendees/players
*Select a bingo prize (will it be cash, a themed basket, a gift certificate or specific item?)

Consider charging $1 per game or offer unlimited games for $20.

As always, adding additional money makers to your event can help raise additional funds for your cause. Add a 50/50 raffle, and/or sell refreshments and food.

SPECIAL NOTE: Be sure your bingo night complies with all local laws and regulations regarding games of chance.

BREAKFAST WITH...

Select a local celebrity, leader or a seasonal figure (i.e. Santa) and invite your community to enjoy breakfast with _____. Sell tickets for $10 in advance or $15 at the door. Serve a breakfast buffet (i.e. biscuits, refreshments, pancakes).

If hosting a breakfast with Santa fundraiser event for your cause, have your volunteer servers dress up as elves. Offer photos with Santa during the event.

If hosting a breakfast with a local celebrity or community leader, ask that they give a short motivational speech during the breakfast.

Add a 50/50 raffle or other raffle items to your event. Be sure to decorate for your event and create a welcoming atmosphere for community members.. Select an inviting location with ample parking and seating. The more attendees, the more funds and awareness you can raise for your organization!

FAMILY FIELD DAY

Family Field Day is a fun event that invites people of all ages to participate for a great cause. Select a spacious outdoor location and begin gathering volunteers several months in advance. Solicit local businesses for donations of prizes for your event (i.e. gift baskets, gift cards). How many prizes will you need? Determine prizes for each category.

Plan the games and events for your event. Below are a few ideas to work with as you get started:

*Wheel barrow race
*Ring toss
*3-legged race (potato sack)
*Horseshoes
*Egg toss
*Corn-hole
*Balloon breaking competition
*Water balloon toss
*Relay race
*Hula-Hoop contest

Consider adding the following to your event:

*Cake walk
*Raffle
*Face painting

Locate a volunteer photographer to capture the fun! Share the photos on your website and social media pages and invite community members to "tag" themselves in the photos (this will allow even more people to view the photos and learn about your cause).

Charge an entry fee (per individual or per family) for your event. Schedule times for each event and provide a sign-up sheet for those who wish to participate.

Volunteers are essential to your success. You will need volunteers to collect admission fees, to operate events and to answer questions about your organization.

HAUNTED TOUR BUS

Speak with your local librarians and/or historians to determine haunted buildings and facilities in your community. Host a haunted tour bus to benefit your organization, during the month of October. Whether your tour bus operates every Saturday, every weekend or one specific weekend - you are sure to draw attention and raise funds for your cause with this unique fundraiser.

Prior to your event, be sure to gain permission from the locations you wish to visit on your bus route. Also, contact your local municipality regarding any restrictions and regulations for commercial driver's licenses. Research bus rental costs and hire a driver.

Who will share information with attendees during your bus tour? Will your local librarian or historian be willing to fill this role? Be sure to have a portable speaker system in place within the bus.

Whether you're hosting your bus tour during the day or evening, it's always fun to schedule a lunch or dinner stop along the way (include the cost of the meal in the price of the admission ticket). Reserve tables in advance.

TIP: Provide attendees with a brochure, pamphlet or souvenir map to include information on each stop.

HAUNTED HOUSE

October brings another great fundraising opportunity for your organization. Host a haunted house and raise funds throughout the entire month. Hold the haunted house event as often as you choose in October.

Where will you host your haunted house? Consider utilizing the home of an employee or volunteer. Or consider hosting a haunted trail or barn (outdoor venue). Once you have selected your ideal location, there is a lot of work to do! Plan ahead and sketch a design plan. What aspects do you wish to exploit in your haunted house? How many volunteers will you need to carry out your plan? What is the total cost of supplies? What will your admission price be? How many tickets do you need to sell to break-even? Do you have proper parking for your venue? How will you advertise your haunted house fundraiser?

Will you have a theme for your haunted house (i.e. Wizard of Oz Haunted House)?

A haunted house fundraiser requires a lot of planning (and a lot of volunteers and decorations), but it is an exciting fundraiser event for your organization. Hosting your haunted house in a unique location (i.e. trail, barn) can draw additional attention – meaning additional guests driving from out-of-town to support your cause.

TRIATHLON

Set a course of running, cycling and swimming. Have participants gain pledges and on the event day they compete to win prizes. Solicit prize donations from local businesses (i.e. gift cards, gift baskets, coupon books, et cetera). Decide how many prizes you will issue (i.e. Top 3 overall males and females).

You will gain donations for your cause through:

1) Participants paying an entry fee to race (Require pre-registration).
2) Participants soliciting pledges from friends and family for their triathlon (i.e. one person pledges $25 to Johnny if he finishes the triathlon event).

*Create pledge sheets for participants. Make it easy for supporters to pledge for an athlete. (Also consider offering online pledge sheets. Create an online participant page for each individual athlete).

*Know your limits. How many athletes can your event allow? Let potential participants know (i.e. *This event is limited to the first 100 athletes who pre-register*).

*Check with your local law enforcement for assistance with traffic control, temporary road closures, and other related issues for your event.

*Plan your start and finish line areas. Make areas spectator friendly.

*Provide ample parking on your event day.

*Additional items you will need:

- Bib/race numbers
- Safety pins (for race numbers)
- Aid stations (and volunteers)
- Doctors/nurses (medical tent)
- Large Clock (for timing the event)
- Cones to designate course areas
- Maps of the course
- Welcome table (for participants to pick up race numbers, course map)
- Volunteers to assist with traffic control and the safety of participants

NOTE: Planning a triathlon course is tricky. Typically events start with swimming. Next, athletes transition into cycling and finish with the running portion of the event. When you plan your course route, work with local professionals (i.e. Race Management Company) for measurements, best course route, et cetera.

MAC & CHEESE FESTIVAL

Who doesn't love macaroni and cheese? With so much love - why not host a fundraiser event focused directly on the delicious food?

This event can be as small or large as you prefer. Invite local community members and businesses to cook up their favorite version of the beloved mac & cheese and attend the festival. Charge an admission fee to raise funds for your cause. A ticket gives you unlimited access to free macaroni and cheese varieties brought in from the public.

Sell refreshments for additional funds.

Ask attendees to stop by a voting booth to cast their vote for the best mac & cheese at the event. Provide a prize to the top three mac & cheese recipes.

MASQUERADE BALL

Dress to the nines and host an evening of elegance, glamor and mystery with a masquerade ball fundraiser!

Begin planning and booking your venue and band a minimum of six months in advance. Many events (especially if you're hosting the event for the first time) may take a year or longer to properly plan and prepare - but it is well worth it!

At minimum, you will need the following:
*Venue
*Plenty of parking
*Band
*Photographer
*Caterer
*Bar
*Decorations committee

Highly Recommended:
*Incorporate a best dressed competition (with prizes awarded).
*Plan your event for a Friday or Saturday evening
*Delegate responsibilities to designated committees (i.e. ticket sales, prize donations, decorations, website and social media publicity, food/wine, expense tracking).
*Create a tag line that shares the purpose of the event. A great example is: "Help Unmask Cancer".
*Host a raffle and/or silent auction with this event.

Consider providing a free printable mask on your website. Bring extra masks and feathers on the night of your event (in case someone forgets or loses their mask).

A masquerade ball is a fun way to bring the community together for a worthy cause. Be sure to clearly state how your organization will utilize funds raised at the event.

WORLD RECORD ATTEMPT

Yes, you can attempt - and possibly set – a world record! It may sound crazy, but it's very possible. Why not spread the word and gather together a large crowd to create the largest game of musical chairs? Invite local news crews, write a press release, and share your goal on social media. The word will spread quickly and garner awareness and attention to your organization and the work that you are doing to help in the local community.

Ask every participant to donate $5 to your charity.

When the big day arrives, send out your last-minute reminders, and enjoy your world record attempt. This is truly a unique experience that the entire community can enjoy (all while raising funds for your cause).

OBSTACLE COURSE CHALLENGE

On your mark. Get set. Go!

An obstacle course challenge can offer an adult course and a kiddie course. Charge participants an entry fee. Solicit donations to be used as prizes for participants. Decide how many prizes you will need (Will you provide a prize to the top male and female? Age categories?).

Hold the obstacle course challenge fundraiser indoors or outdoors, depending on the weather conditions and options available in your area. If you are hosting your event outdoors, be sure to check with your local parks department and municipality regarding regulations.

Determine the length of the obstacle course. Be sure to have a clear start and finish line. Will your starting line allow for all participants to begin at the same time? Or will you need to provide a staggered start? Will participants wear timing chips or will you manually time? Be prepared with plenty of volunteers for this event.

Determining the obstacles for the event is exciting. Below, you will find a few ideas to get you started:

*Tire push
*Log roll
*Rope climbs
*Overhead ladders
*Carry a weighed backpack

*Balance beam
*Army crawl

GAMBLING NIGHT

Set up a variety of tables (i.e. poker) for a successful casino night fundraiser.

What you will need:

*Locate corporate sponsors for each casino night table (the sponsorship should cover the general cost of the table). Provide a large sign for the corporate sponsor, at each table. Encourage corporate sponsors to supply small free gifts (given to attendees to help advertise their business).
*Plenty of volunteers! (i.e. Welcome table, Dealers).
*Determine your ticket price. Know how many tickets your organization needs to sell to break even. Select a volunteer committee to help with ticket sales (i.e. ask each committee member to sell a minimum of 20 tickets each).
*Keep track of your expenses! It's easy to spend quickly…but remember, you are hosting this event to raise funds for your cause.
*Designate a decorating committee for your event.
*Where will you rent your casino equipment?
*Consider hiring professional dealers (volunteers may be able to staff some of the easier tables such as blackjack).
*Purchase insurance.
*Will you hire security?
*Decide if alcohol is included in the price of the admission ticket.
*All volunteers and hired employees for the event should wear the same attire.

*Hire an emcee for your event to announce raffle prizes, et cetera.

IMPORTANT: Check your local laws and speak with your municipality regarding regulations, prior to the event. You must also check with your State Gaming Commission and/or the Attorney General's office.

MUD VOLLEYBALL TOURNAMENT

When hosting a *mud* volleyball tournament it is especially important to choose the right location (and the right time of year) for your event. Be sure that the venue is aware of your intentions (creating mud volleyball courts). In addition to a great location, you will also need to create and manage brackets, coordinate teams and players, and manage officials and spectators.

Charge a registration fee (it's a good idea to require pre-registration, so that you are properly prepared on tournament day). Will you require team registration? Or can individuals register (and you place them on a team)? Will teams be co-ed? Will you have a game time limit? Determine the rules for your tournament.

Select a location with room for two regulation size courts, minimum. If you plan on hosting the event as an annual fundraiser, the size of your venue may need to expand each year.

Can you find equipment to rent (or better yet, donated) for your event (i.e. volleyball nets)? Will you rent bleachers for spectators or ask that they bring their own chairs?

Will you sell food and refreshments to raise additional funds on tournament day? Be prepared with plenty of volunteers to assist.

Select qualified and knowledgeable volunteers to keep score of the games.

Designate a prize committee prior to the event. The prize committee should collect donated prizes to provide to the winning tournament team members.

To create the mud volleyball courts you will need several hoses. Remove the sod (approximately 12 inches deep) and fill with water.

HINT: Keep hoses on hand for participants to clean themselves up after games.

POLAR PLUNGE

Round up willing participants to take part in your polar plunge for charity event. Participants collect pledges for taking the plunge.

Polar Plunge fundraisers are generally held in the winter months. Consider renting a venue near the water, for participants (and spectators) to warm up after the plunge (Have extra towels and warmers on hand). You may also want to host a pancake breakfast following the plunge.

TIP: It is good practice to keep a doctor, nurse and/or medical professionals on hand. Have participants sign a liability waiver prior to your event. Talk to your insurance professional regarding coverage.

A TRULY NOVEL AFFAIR

Invite local authors to attend an exclusive book signing at your local library or rented venue. Sell tickets to your event to raise funds for your cause. The ticket price can include wine (or a wine tasting) and other refreshments. You may also consider including a dinner with the ticket price. If you hold a dinner, ask authors to speak while attendees are enjoying their meals.

As with any large event, be sure to spread the word. The more tickets you sell, the more funds you will raise for your cause. Spread the word to local libraries, book clubs, schools, universities, and more.

When you pair this event with a dinner and/or wine tasting, you'll gain an even larger turn-out.

Authors should bring a selection of their books. Hire an emcee and provide several raffles of free books (or book packages or a Kindle reader) to attendees, throughout the evening. (Also invite attendees to bring their pre-purchased books for attending authors to sign).

RELAY FOR LIFE

Invite teams of 10-12 individuals to complete a long run/walk (i.e. 8-hours). Teams pay $100-$200 to register. Teams will also gather pledges to raise additional funds for the cause.

Hold your run/walk on a track or on a trail loop. Designate the run/walk area and clearly mark.

You will need plenty of volunteers on hand for event day. At minimum, volunteers will need to help with:

*Welcoming teams (providing race/bib numbers, t-shirts)
*Aid stands (providing calories/hydration to participants)
*Announcing (during the event announce fun facts about participants, the charity and more)
*Music (radio, local musicians/bands)- help participants stay motivated!
*Plenty of water, Gatorade, bananas, et cetera.

Be sure to have medical professionals on hand throughout the event (have a medical tent set up). Purchase insurance for your event and have participants sign a liability waiver prior to beginning their run/walk.

Invite local news and radio hosts to visit your event. Designate a spokesperson for your charity.

Remember, in this event, everyone is a winner. Provide every participant who finishes the pre-determined relay time with a finishers medal or award.

SUMMER SOCIAL

Host a luncheon on the grounds of a local Victorian mansion. After obtaining the appropriate approvals, determine your menu. Hire a professional caterer for your event. It is beneficial to locate a local historian to volunteer his/her time to attend the luncheon and provide interesting information on the local grounds/mansions, to attendees.

Following the luncheon, are you able to score a guided tour of the mansion? If so, by all means, do it! This is a fun and unique fundraiser for your cause.

ANTIQUE SHOW

Come one, come all - to the antique show!

Begin planning and collecting antique items one year in advance. The more items you collect, the more items you can sell--- meaning the more money you can raise for your charity.

1) Secure a spacious location (remember to have plenty of parking available!)

2) Collect antique items throughout the year.

3) Offer a preview party prior to the big event. Hold the preview party several hours before the event or the day before your event.

4) Sell the antique items at your event. Before the event, decide if you will price the items with tags or if you will ask attendees to make offers on the items.

There are a variety of ways to host your event. Consider charging an admission fee and providing refreshments and finger foods throughout the event. Or you can forego the admission fee and simply raise funds by selling the antique items at your show. Either way, you will raise significant funds for your cause.

EVENING AS A CHILD

Play is an important aspect of life and one that is often overlooked by grown adults. But when you host an "Evening as a Child" fundraiser, you'll find that we're all still kids at heart! This event requires adults to pay an admission fee. Fill the venue with kids activities for adults to participate in (i.e. tricycle race, wheelbarrow race, monkey bar challenge, jump rope competition).

Have a prize ready for each event winner. Offer a 50/50 raffle to raise additional funds.

As with most large events, consider hiring a photographer to capture the fun. It is also beneficial to select a volunteer committee/team to help organize the event. What activities will you offer? How will you advertise your event? What props do you need for each activity? This event requires a group of volunteers to act as event judges, as well.

Invite a local band/musician to play at your event and/or invite an emcee to add a bit of pizzazz!

FESTIVAL OF TREES

The National Christmas Tree Association (yes, this is a real thing!) reports that 20-30 million real Christmas trees are sold annually in the United States. (The Association also explains that for every real Christmas tree harvested, 1 to 3 seedlings are planted the following spring). Naturally, when trees are purchased, the next step is to bring them home and decorate.

With so many holiday trees being sold each year, why not offer a pre-decorated tree sale to raise funds for your charity? Spare buyers from decorating the tree and raise funds for a great cause. Offer pre-decorated real trees or artificial trees – or both!

Collaborate with a local business (preferably one with a large parking lot and a lot of traffic) to utilize their outdoor space for your fundraiser. Sell your pre-decorated holiday trees every weekend in December to raise maximum funds for your cause.

LEAP OF LOVE

Literally take a LEAP for your organization with this Leap of Love fundraising event. Invite teams of 20 for a leap-frog championship. Organize a one-mile course and charge an entry fee. The event works best if you have a minimum of 20 teams.

Keep in mind that you will need plenty of volunteers to assist with this event. Volunteers can assist with gathering teams for the event, setting up the course, directing participants to stay on course, hosting an aid station, tracking finishing times of each team, et cetera.

Invite a local musician/band to play at your event. Spread the word to local news and radio stations, as well.

Provide a prize to the top team (remember, with teams of 20, you will need 20 prizes to award!).

HINT: Pair this event with a bake sale to raise maximum funds.

FIELD OF DREAMERS

Rent a baseball field or stadium for the day. Find retired or off-season baseball players (or local celebrities) to participate.

Invite the public to "Pay to Play" baseball with _____ *(fill in the player or celebrities name here)*. Advertise what positions are available to play (i.e. right field, bat boy, umpire, et cetera) and charge a pay to play fee for each participant.

Once you have your team organized (don't forget to invite benchwarmers, too!), you can order matching shirts with your organization's logo, the participants last name and an assigned number. The shirts will serve as a great marketing tool for your cause, even after the event has passed.

On event day, invite spectators and charge a $5 admission fee. Volunteers from your organization can host a food/refreshment stand to sell items to raise even more funds.

TIP: If your organization has a mascot, consider bringing him/her along to take photos with the kiddos during the event!

BLACK TIE DINNER, WITH YOUR PET(S)

This event works best when dogs are the invited guests (cats are usually homebodies and are a little tricky!). The fundraiser is great for animal welfare organizations, but can work well with any cause. We are a nation that loves our pets and bringing them along to a fancy dinner is a unique opportunity for pets and their guardians to enjoy a fun night out.

This event requires a lot of preparation and planning. Below is a list of a few things to offer at your event:

*A sign for "doggie restrooms" (directing guests to a well-lit outdoor area).
*Doggie appetizers.
*Doggie water bowls (strategically placed around the venue for easy access).
*Plenty of seating for humans. Catered appetizers, dinner, dessert and drinks.
*Live music/entertainment.
*Silent auction and/or live auction items. Raffles.
*Photographer(s).

When you reserve your banquet hall/venue for your event, be sure to confirm that dogs are okay.

Purchase insurance for your event.

This event will raise significant funds for your charity. Charge an admission fee for each human. You will raise additional funds through silent and live auction items and raffles. Don't forget to designate several committees for your event (i.e. decorating committee, silent auction items committee, music committee, food/drink committee, welcome committee, ticket sales committee, and more).

MURDER MYSTERY DINNER

Host a *killer* fundraiser for your cause. Murder Mystery dinners raise funds for your charity through collecting an admission fee. The event generally takes three hours to complete (this includes dinner). Host this event with 10-200 people.

Consider the following when planning your big event:

*Where will you hold the event (i.e. in a volunteer's home? A rented venue?)?
*Will dinner be catered or prepared by volunteers?
*What will you charge per ticket? How many tickets must you sell to make a profit?
*What is your budget? Select a committee to track expenses.
*Designate committees to plan for: decorating/theme, invitations, costumes, webpage/ticket sales, advertising, et cetera.

Prepare your murder mystery scenario prior to the big event. Who will turn up missing? What clues will be left to help attendees attempt to figure it all out?

Don't forget to have a special prize ready for the winner of your murder mystery dinner.

Consider selling t-shirts with your organizations logo and the event name and year. Shirt sales will help raise additional funds and be an ongoing advertisement for your cause.

HINT: A good reference when planning your event is the classic mystery game, *Clue*. While playing *Clue,* players attempt to find the murderer, where the murder occurred and what weapon was used.

CLASSIC CAR SHOW

Ladies and Gentlemen, start your engines…

Select a large outdoor venue with ample parking and set the mood. For a classic car show (you can choose any theme you would like), invite attendees to dress in period clothing. It's time to go old-school for a great cause.

Charge an admission fee. Sell food/refreshments at your event to raise additional funds.

Hire a local musician/band for live entertainment (play music matching the time period of cars on showcase).

Invite corporate sponsors to take part in your event. In return, supply your sponsors with professional advertising.

Where do you get cars for your show? Start early (at least one year in advance). Invite the public to bring their classic cars to the show. Contact your local car club or locate a local non-profit organization that has a focus on classic cars.

Don't forget to purchase insurance and keep track of your budget!

Make your event an extravaganza. Held annually, your event will grow each year as the word continues to spread. This event is about having fun and enjoying classic cars. Know your goal, spread the word like crazy and enjoy the event while raising massive funds for your organization.

DOG SHOW

Bark for the cause! This fundraiser works great for animal welfare related charities, but it can also bring in ample funds for other groups, too. How does it work? Showcase shelter/rescue dogs who are ready for adoption. You'll be raising money for your cause and promoting local adoptable dogs.

Tips:

*Have a runway at your event to showcase the adoptable dogs.
*Show the dogs in categories (small, medium and large breeds).
*Work with a local groomer(s) to prepare the dogs for the big day!
*Use cute bandannas or bows to dress up the dogs.
*Be prepared - have plenty of water bowls and snacks for participating dogs. Don't forget your volunteers— have more than you think you will need. Volunteers will need to assist with ticket sales, welcoming, seating, walking the dogs, caring for/monitoring the dogs, et cetera.
*Hire an emcee for the event (the emcee can announce fun facts about each dog as he/she is walked - or carried - down the runway).
*Be prepared for adoptions (have adoption coordinators on hand to assist).
*Don't forget the music!
*Be patient - some dogs will be nervous or timid. Be sure to have professional assistance on hand (i.e. rescue professionals, veterinarians).

*Hire or locate a volunteer photographer for the event.
*Sell dog themed items at your event to raise additional funds (i.e. dog treats, dog bandanas, dog books, t-shirts with your organization's logo and the event name and year, et cetera).
*Invite your local news and radio teams to attend the event. Utilize press releases two-weeks prior to your event.
*Offer plenty of seating for guests. Will the price of admission include refreshments and food or will you offer those items separately for purchase?
*Purchase insurance.

Hosting a dog show is a great way to bring the community together. In the United States, animal shelters kill more than three to four million companion animals annually. Promote local pet adoption with this entertaining event, and raise monumental funds for a great cause while doing so.

BRICKS

Pave your way to profits! Locate a local service that will provide individual personalized bronze plaques for your bricks. Create a brick walkway to the entrance of your organization. Ask donors to provide a $500 or larger donation to "purchase a personalized brick" for the cause. This will be an ongoing fundraiser for your charity.

For every donation of $500 or more, your organization adds a personalized brick to the new walkway. Ask what information the donor would like included on their brick (names, quote, et cetera). This is a special way to recognize and encourage large donations.

MUST DO'S FOR BIG EVENTS

Once you've decided on a specific large fundraiser event for your organization, it's time to get to work. Event location is imperative to your success. Before you move ahead, consider the following:

- Where will you host your event?
- Is the location easily accessible to attendees?
- Will ample parking space be available?
- If the event will be held in the evening, does the parking lot provide proper lighting?
- Are most people familiar with the location?
- Will you provide a map and specific directions to attendees? Do you have a contact number for attendees to call if they are lost?
- Is your location visually appealing (welcoming) on the outside and inside of the facility?

Once you've pinned down a proper location for the event, you can move forward with the planning.

Gather a team or committee of volunteers to assist you in focusing on this specific event. Assign roles to each volunteer. Appoint a group of people to be in charge of hiring the emcee and musician(s) for your event, for example. Providing volunteers with specific tasks will help your event planning. The event coordinator should schedule regular check-in's with each volunteer, to help keep everyone motivated and focused (and to help address any frustrations that may arise along the way).

Every event is unique to the organization that it serves. Most large-scale events may consider inviting corporate sponsors. The expense sheet can quickly add up when planning an event. A corporate sponsor can help offset costs for your fundraiser. Ask corporate sponsors to donate a specific amount and in return, they are provided with promotional advertising at your event. For example, you may host an annual wine tasting event for your organization. If you gain a $100 corporate sponsor from a local business, you can offer that sponsor a full-color ad in your event program and feature their logo on the front page of your website during the month of your event. Of course, corporate sponsor amounts and offerings can vary, depending on the nature of your event and the amount of traffic you can bring to a corporate sponsor. While corporate sponsorships are often given out of philanthropy, businesses are also looking for something in return for the funds supplied. When you are able to create value for sponsorships your organization will reap the benefits of your efforts.

All fundraisers require planning. With large events, generally planning will take nine-months or longer. Although this may seem like a lot of time, there is a lot of work to do. Creating a specific plan and assigning detailed tasks are essential to putting together a successful event. Don't get discouraged! Planning ahead and providing yourself with months of preparation time will prove helpful on event day.

Planning, focus and consistency are important points to remember during the process. When the big fundraiser day arrives you will be glad you put in the time and effort and you will enjoy being a part of an astonishing event. Being part of a well-planned event that benefits a worthy cause is truly an amazing experience.

HOW TO SELL TICKETS

You've decided on your big event. You have your location. You've been planning for months. You have an emcee, musicians, beautiful décor and an entertaining event planned. So, how do you sell tickets?

Social Media
Utilize a free form of advertising by reaching out to your supporters on social media. Create a Facebook event page and send direct invites.

Email
If you're hosting a large fundraiser event, you should already have a robust list of long-time supporters and donors for your organization. Send out a friendly e-mail to inform them about the event. Let them know the details of the event and specifically how the event will benefit your organization and what they can expect if they attend.

Newsletter
If your organization produces a regular newsletter, place a full-page ad in the newsletter (or an article) with the details of the event and a website address or phone number contact where those interested can obtain additional information.

Website
Place a notice on the front page of your website (generally begin 3-4 weeks prior to your event and continue until the event takes place). It is also highly

recommended that you create a specific page within your website for the event (where tickets are directly purchased online).

Flyers
Create eye-catching flyers and post them around your city (i.e. grocery stores, library). Ask local businesses to hang your event flyer in their lobbies or front doors, as well. This can get people talking about your event and more importantly, help you sell more tickets.

Mail Invites
Yes, good old-fashioned mail can work wonders! Do you want to stand out from the crowd? Send a postcard to invite your supporters to attend the event. When sending invites via mail, be sure to specifically target those who may be interested in attending your event (don't blindly mail them to every address in one neighborhood).

Start Early
Planning for a large event takes time, dedication and a lot of effort. You can never start too early.
Consider giving yourself 9-12 months to plan a large- scale event. First you will want to secure a location and date for your event; then, let the planning begin!

Utilize your volunteers and supporters networks
Create excitement among your volunteers and supporters! If you're excited about the event, most likely others will be, too. Check in with your

volunteers: can they announce the event at their place of employment? Can they help hang flyers? Can they share posts on their social media pages to help spread the word? Reaching out to other networks can only help to improve attendance at your event.

Follow up on invitations
Keep a list of who you've sent invitations. If those you have invited have not purchased a ticket two-weeks prior to your event, call or e-mail with a follow-up. Often people become busy and forget to purchase their tickets (while they have every intention of doing so). Doing a quick and friendly follow-up can yield additional ticket sales with minimal effort.

Sell to groups
Offer group discounts. For example, offer a 5% discount on ticket sales to the Young Professionals organization in your city. Or you can offer a special rate to a specific group if 10 or more tickets are purchased from that group. Get creative; it will pay off!

Corporate Sponsorships
When offering corporate sponsorships for your event, consider including free tickets. For example, if your organization offers a corporate sponsorship for $500, what will you do for the corporation in return? What are they getting for their money (other than knowing they are supporting a great cause)? In addition to offering the business free advertising space on the front page of your website and in your event program, why not offer a number of free tickets, too? By

offering tickets, you may gain additional support and donations.

V.I.P.
Consider offering an exclusive V.I.P section or table at your event. Attendees pay a higher ticket price to sit at the V.I.P. table.

Members Only Pre-Sale
If you have a large number of supporters, offering an exclusive members only pre-sale is a great way to drum up additional ticket sales and donations for your event.

Add Pizzazz
Excitement is contagious! When you're excited about your event, that energy will shine through and others will catch on to the excitement (which means they will be more likely to purchase tickets and spread the word to their friends, family and co-workers).

You can also add pizzazz to your event in any number of ways. Below are a few ideas:

*Create your event around a fun theme.
*Offer a several exciting door prizes or auction items at the event.
*Have a motivational speaker at your event.
*Feature a local band.
*Coordinate an appearance by a local celebrity (add this to the headline of your event).

*Have a large raffle item (i.e. vehicle). Announce the winner the night of your event (winner must be present to win).

Make it easy to purchase tickets

Offer a BUY NOW button on your website. Make purchasing tickets to your event quick and easy. Not only should your event be indicated and easily visible on your websites home page, it should also have its own webpage within your site (including event details and a BUY NOW button for tickets).

Offer a Giveaway (i.e. free tickets)

If you need to raise your attendance level, give-away tickets. Now you're asking, *but how will I make money?* Remember, you're not giving away all of your tickets, just a few. And when you increase attendance, the appeal of the event grows. People love to see why there is a crowd. So, how do you give away tickets? Below are a few examples:

*If you give-away tickets to a concert, sell beverages (you will more than make up your money here).
*Host a social media contest. For example "re-tweet for a chance to win tickets" (*Twitter*) or "Pin it to win it" (*Pinterest*).
*Offer Buy One, Get One for tickets purchased during a specific week.
*Host an online quiz on a social media site or your website. Ask a question pertaining to your organization; the first five people to answer correctly win a set of free tickets to your event.

*Offer an incentive. If your supporters/volunteers sell twenty tickets to your event, they get two free.

Create urgency for ticket sales
Urgency creates action. Set a deadline for ticket purchases. Use wording such as:

"Must purchase by..."

"Limited tickets available..."

"Buy your tickets before it's too late!"

Pricing
In real estate, it's all about location. With fundraising events it's all about price point. Set your ticket price too high, you'll risk losing potential attendees. Set your ticket price too low and you may tarnish the image of an elegant event.

First, keep track of your expenses for the event. What are your total costs? How many attendees do you realistically expect to attend? What ticket price (and what number of ticket sales) will allow you to break even on your event? What ticket price will allow you to profit?

Survey other fundraising events in your local area; other groups and non-profits most likely have held galas and other large fundraising events. What were their ticket prices? What did they offer for the price? How many attendees did they have? Do they have a similar size supporter base?

There is a lot to consider when setting the ticket price for your big event. It is also important to keep in mind how many tickets you plan to give-away. Remember, you're planning this event to *raise* money for your organization.

Offer Contests

Contests can add additional incentive for ticket purchases. Why not offer a raffle for those who buy tickets prior to a specific date? The winner of the raffle could sit at a V.I.P. table, for example.

You can also offer a special gift to the first twenty ticket purchasers (given at the event).

Utilizing contests to enhance ticket sales is a creative and fun way to draw attention to your big event.

THE MAGIC WORDS

Don't forget to say THANK YOU to your attendees, donors and supporters. A simple in-person thank you goes a long way. Attendees of your event want to know that they're helping make a difference. They are attending because they believe in the organization's mission. Let them know how their support is helping create a genuine difference in your local community.

In addition to offering a sincere in-person thank you to attendees, you may also consider offering your thanks in any number of creative ways. Below are a few examples:

*Send a snail mail, hand-written thank you card.
*Post a thank you on your social media pages.
*List donor names in your event program.
*Announce donor names during your event.
*Provide event attendees with a special thank you gift.

THANK YOU!

Thank you for choosing to read *Fun(d)raising: 150 Money Making Ideas.* I hope you've found the information and ideas in this book beneficial for your organization. Most of all, thank you for the work that you do in your community. The world needs you and we are lucky to have you!

Much gratitude to everyone at Rockville Publishing and to my wonderful editors Eve Elephante and Gloria Rayle. I'm still buzzing with excitement about this book! I'm looking forward to our future collaborations on fundraising events for charities near and dear to our hearts. Thank you for believing in my vision and for your unwavering support with this and other books.

I believe in the beauty of following your heart and in doing work that creates value in our communities. Of course, if that were simple, everyone would do it. Being brave enough to hone your talent and follow your passion is commendable. If you are one of the many brave souls who have started, volunteer or work for a non-profit organization, school or other worthy cause - THANK YOU. Now it's time to use the ideas and principles you have learned throughout the book and get to work. Organizations need funds to continue operating. Let's start planning and when you host a new successful fundraiser for your group, please be sure to leave an **AMAZON REVIEW** and let me know how it goes. I want to know what events are working for your organization and how you've tailored those events to your program or theme. When we share our experiences with each other, we can help other worthy causes in their endeavors to assist the world, too.

REVIEWS ARE SO IMPORTANT

If *Fun(d)raising: 150 Money Making Ideas* was helpful to you, an Amazon Review is much appreciated.

ABOUT THE AUTHOR

Stacey Ritz is an award-winning writer, author and blogger. For more than a decade Ritz has served as the Executive Director and is the co-founder of Advocates 4 Animals, Inc. – a 501(c)3 non-profit organization. With a degree in Business Marketing and a Master's in Education, Stacey strives to share her marketing and fundraising experience and expertise with other groups who are working to improve their local communities.

Ritz chronicles her quirky unconventional life as an advocate for cats (and all animals) in her books and blogs. She often finds herself perplexed in the midst of comical situations that warrant sharing- many stories of which you can find on her Kitties in the City blog (www.kittiesinthecity.com). Stac, as she's most often called, recently realized, spelled backwards, her name is "cats". Ironic? Maybe not.

Books by Stacey Ritz

Pawsitive Connection:
Heartwarming Stories of Animals Finding People
When We Need Them Most - Volume I

Cat Connection:
Heartwarming Rescue Tales – Volume II

Letters from Cats:
Hilarious & Heartfelt Notes

Covered in Pet Fur:
How to Start an Animal Rescue, The Right Way

Fun(d)raising:
150 Money Making Ideas

Covered in
Pet Fur

How to Start an Animal Rescue
The Right Way

STACEY RITZ *and* **AMY BEATTY**
Founders of Advocates 4 Animals

YOUR FREE SAMPLE OF

COVERED IN PET FUR...

FORWARD

IT SAT IN A FORGOTTEN PART OF THE CITY. The dilapidated building was dark and surrounded by an eight foot tall barbed wire fence. The only sign was no larger than a sheet of computer paper. It was crookedly suspended, hanging from one rotting corner just above the padlock. It read "OPEN HOURS" and any remaining words had been long since bleached by the relentless sun. I double checked the address on my sheet of paper. (This was before I owned a cell phone and I had never dreamed that one day we would have GPS systems leading us anywhere we desired to go.) It was the correct address. But weren't animal shelters supposed to be friendly places filled with people who adored animals? Weren't non-profit organizations supposed to be clean and welcoming? Weren't they there to help? My mind buzzed with questions, although neither of us said a word. We were still in undergraduate school learning the ways of the world. Yet we had no idea we were about to embark on one of our most impactful lessons as we hesitantly approached the padlocked gates.

A burley man in a blue and black checkered flannel vest strolled out to the fence from inside, a worn cigarette hanging from the left corner of his mouth as a cloud of smoke surrounded his solemn face. I admit I wanted to turn and run back to the safety of our car. But my curiosity got the best of me. Or maybe we were both just paralyzed; in shock from our new surroundings. We were accustomed to our plush college campus, bright lights, clean sidewalks, smiling faces…but somehow we had driven ourselves just a few miles away into what felt like the Twilight Zone. Maybe now, well over a decade later, I would have turned and run. No seriously, who I am kidding? I would have stayed. I wanted to know what was behind the barbed wire. I wanted to know what happened to the animals who were found being abused, who were no longer wanted through no fault of their own. I wanted to know the reality of life for companion animals in our country. And although we spent years volunteering at various shelters, pounds and sanctuaries around the Midwest, I attribute what we have built today to our first day at this particular shelter; where countless lives were tossed into the dark and left, forgotten by the rest of the world. *Out of sight, out of mind.*

We located the shelter address through the phone book. I am well aware that this dates us, as we were living in a pre-Google time. But maybe what saved us was my chatter. I'll never be sure, but back in those days I tended to ramble when my nerves got the best of me. It was my own way of trying to calm myself. Whatever it was, the flannelled man we came to know as Todd pulled out his key and allowed us through the gates and into the city shelter. Our bewildered faces tried to take it all in. When we explained that we wanted to volunteer, Todd raised his eyebrows as if to indicate that we must be crazy. He explained that he did not have any open paid positions, not understanding why anyone would subject themselves to this environment without receiving a paycheck. We told him we just wanted to spend time with the animals, to bring in toys for the cats, to take the dogs on walks; we just wanted to give them some love and attention while they waited behind bars for a slim chance at finding a home. Todd nodded, clearly thinking we would never return.

First, Todd led us to a narrow building they called "the cat room". Small rusty wire cages were piled from floor to ceiling and stacked side by side. Only a slender opening existed down the center of the piles of cages leaving a space for us to walk. No one was spayed or neutered. No one was vaccinated. A few animals had food in their cages, hardly any had water and the bowls looked as if they had been dry for quite some time. No one had toys and most of the litter boxes were overflowing with old feces. Many cats started meowing when we entered the room, some stuck their paws through the wire bars, begging for help. My initial reaction was to run and open every cage door and let them all run free in the room while we scrambled to clean their cages and fill their bowls with fresh food and water and their crates with toys and clean litter. But instead I pressed my hands behind my back and tried to remain calm. We asked questions about how many adoptions they had, why absolutely no vetting was supplied to the pets in their care and we learned that there had never been volunteers. *Never.*

Next we walked over to the main building. The room looked to be caving in and the small space was dark. No natural light existed. It looked more like an old barn than a shelter. There was no heating or air conditioning, just cages stacked in endless rows, filled with dogs of every color and size. Most of them couldn't stand up in their cages without having to hunch down in their cramped quarters. The dogs never left their crates unless by some odd stroke of luck they were adopted by a rare visitor. Todd said the only other way the dogs ever left their cages happened to be if they died in their crates, and that happened too often. There were six long rows of wire dog crates lining what we grew to call The Warehouse. The crates were stacked on top of each other, just as the cats had been. Only with the dogs, some small dogs were caged next to large dogs and they fought viciously through the bent metal bars, frustrated by their helpless fates. It was enough to rattle even the most placid visitors. It wasn't until months later that we would learn of a "secret room" in a back building where additional dogs were held in the dark. This building was more like a shed. Like The Warehouse it had no natural light, but to make matters worse, there was no electricity and the cage floors had rotted, leaving the dogs behind bars often yelping in pain as their paws fell through the rotted holes in the floor boards.

We began volunteering once a week and then twice. Every free moment we had outside of classes, studies and our training and competitions for the indoor track, outdoor track and cross country team we found ourselves driving to the forgotten corner of town and spending hours upon hours with the imprisoned animals.

Todd left us to our own devices. He stayed in his small building off to the side from the others. We would always stop in and say good-bye as we left each time and he would be leaning back in his chair puffing away on that old cigarette. As ghastly as it may sound, more than a decade and a half later, Todd is still the most compassionate open intake shelter or pound director we have met to date. I wish it wasn't so, but Todd shines above the others we would meet as time marched on. Compassion, among other things, somehow is always missing in our nation's city shelter and county pound directors. Job requirements tend to be focused on obedience and adherence to the random stipulations of keeping the cages empty at all costs, rather than trying to help the animals that the facility should be there to serve and protect.

By our second visit to the dilapidated shelter, we had opened every cat cage in the room, letting them run free. The cats had a window and each took turns looking out into the world, some perhaps for the first time in years. A few cats jumped on top of the long heavy lights hanging from the ceiling and knowing they were happy to move around, we laughed in delight. We made hundreds of toys so that every cage had several variations to help numb the sting of solitude when they were locked back up and we were away. Each visit we thoroughly cleaned every litter box and gave them fresh food and water. We lined their wire crates with newspaper so that their paws could find a soft place to land (we would collect old newspapers and bring them with us). We were college students and didn't have much extra money, but when we had some to spare we would buy treats to give the cats on our visits. In time we developed a system where every visit, we let ten cats out of their cages at a time to play, rotating until everyone had a taste of freedom for the day. On rare occasion Todd would walk over to the small building and crack the door open to ask if everything was going okay. He may have thought we were crazy, two twenty-year olds spending our free time playing with cats; but we didn't think a thing about it. We were exactly where we wanted to be.

After spending half of the day with the cats, we would move on to the dogs. For the first few months of volunteering we would choose five dogs to walk at once. We would secure them into collars and leashes and take off into the city surrounded by fast moving cars with tinted windows and booming music, and strolling through deserted parks. We would walk the group of dogs for a mile or so and head back for another batch. We walked Pit-Bulls and Rottweiler's, Chihuahua's and mixed breeds. At the time we didn't know the labels given to any of the breeds; we only knew that they needed exercise and fresh air. We knew intuitively that they needed love.

Eventually we discovered a large fenced area in the back of the buildings. The grass was tall and the area had clearly never been used. *Another forgotten place.* Our young minds saw the unused space as an opportunity. That very day, without asking permission, we giggled like children as we took the dogs from their unsightly cages one by one and released them into the fenced back yard. After an hour we had every dog from the shelter out in the yard together. It never occurred to us that some dogs may not get along with others. It never crossed our minds that most of the dogs were unaltered. We only knew we wanted them to experience life, rather than to simply rot away in the forgotten building. If we could bring them one good day, we knew they would be happier for it. We didn't have any dog toys, but we found old branches and tossed them to the larger dogs. We kneeled on the ground to pet the small and senior canines and our eyes danced as we watched every one of them trot and run in the forgotten space, taking in the fresh air that touched their bodies, some for the first time in years. Todd wandered out into the yard after hearing our shouts of play and I turned just in time to see him shake his head, that darn cigarette hanging permanently from the corner of his mouth. Before I could blink, he had disappeared back into his office and we continued to play.

In all of our years at the shelter, we continued the tradition of letting the dogs run free together in the yard while we played with them and gave them attention (and we did the same for the cat room). Never once did we encounter an altercation between the dogs. They loved the sweet taste of freedom and it was clear that they weren't going to do anything to lose those moments of rare bliss.

During our last two years of undergraduate school, we scheduled a date once a year where the entire women's track team came to volunteer at the city animal shelter. Some spent time with cats and others helped walk the dogs throughout the city.

We continued volunteering several times a week as the years marched on and we grew closer to earning our degrees. We flew to Stanford, rode charter buses to Duke and everywhere in between for our competitive races (track and cross country) and each time we returned, we found ourselves covered in pet fur in a forgotten corner of the city. One day as we entered the cat room, we noticed an elderly cat who stood motionless in her rusty cage, a malnourished kitten draped lifelessly over her boney back. The older cat had long brittle gray fur that fell off in clumps with each new breath. One eye held steady on us, the other was missing and left in its place was a socket full of fresh oozing blood and infection. We reached in to hold her and felt every bone in her frail body. The little beige kitten wasn't fairing any better. We carried them across the gravel yard and into Todd's office to ask about them. Where had they come from? What happened to the older ones eye? Couldn't they get some veterinary care? By that point we had been talking with veterinarians in the area to see if they would be willing to donate some of their time to the forgotten shelter. We were dismissed as "dumb kids" time and again, until one veterinarian said *maybe*. That maybe got us fired up. We pitched the idea to Todd and he said it wasn't possible. We tried time and again to bring veterinarians to the shelter. We offered to drive shelter pets to the veterinarian's office. We offered everything we could think of to allow the shelter pets to be provided at least the minimal forms of veterinary care, but our efforts were to no avail.

The frail, elderly one-eyed gray cat had been turned in a few days before, Todd explained. Their best guess was that someone had purposely gouged her eye out. The kitten who was with her wasn't hers; they just didn't have anywhere else to place him. And so the two numb souls sat huddled together in a bottom cage, waiting for…nothing. No veterinary care was coming. No one would adopt either sick cat. They were simply waiting to rot away like the building itself had been doing for years before our arrival.

"Could we adopt them?" I blurted out instinctively. Todd shrugged his shoulders nonchalantly.

"Sure, just need to see your driver's license. That old one, she won't make it another night." He took a long puff of his cigarette as he filled out a yellowed piece of paper. "You can have her for free. She'll never make it."

We clung to the two cats, knowing if we adopted them, we could take them in for desperately needed veterinary care. And a minute later, we found ourselves saving our first two shelter cats – embarking on what would soon evolve into Advocates 4 Animals, Inc.

We named the elderly gray cat Princess. After taking the frail cat to a veterinarian and spending $500 on surgery for her gouged eye, my parents stopped talking to me. Clearly unhappy with how I choose to spend the minimal money I had as a college student, they shook their heads in disapproval. A month later we shelled out a few hundred dollars more for Princess as it was discovered her uterus was falling apart internally. We had her spayed and vaccinated and each day she grew stronger. Her hair grew in healthy and full, she threw her tail in the air as she trotted through the house and after more than a month of coaxing her to eat, she finally began eating on her own. Her emaciated 4-pound adult body grew into a healthy 12-pounds. Princess inspired our logo for Advocates 4 Animals and despite all that she had endured, despite the dire warning Todd had given us that Princess would not last one more night, she lived 10 more years.

Sadly the kitten we saved with her passed away within a week. In his severely malnourished state, he had been given a strong dose of adult flea preventative at the shelter, which had ultimately killed him. Although no vetting was provided at the shelter, the flea medications had been delivered as a promotion and shelter workers had not been versed on how to administer the medications (the adult version was too strong for his weak kitten body).

We saved a handful of others from that particular shelter prior to moving away from the city after college graduation, and we hung posters and flyers on every free light post and telephone pole encouraging others to adopt a rescue pet as well. Adoptions at the shelter saw an increase and we were pleased knowing that this was a step forward. Sadly, the shelter never forged a relationship with a veterinarian. Todd left the shelter the year after we had graduated and moved out of state. A few years later we learned that the forgotten shelter had been condemned. As for us, we continued leading a life covered in pet fur. After countless years spent volunteering in shelters, pounds, sanctuaries and working at various veterinary hospitals, kennels and operating a pet-sitting business we pressed on to co-found an organization that existed to specifically help shelter pets in need. We set out to reform the shelter system. We were two girls on a mission of compassion, a mission of humane treatment for the millions of voiceless victims needlessly dying in shelters and pounds each year through no fault of their own. And today, that mentality hasn't changed. We're still two girls, albeit a bit older now, on a mission to transform the grim reality of shelter pets into one of a reality of thriving existence. We're still fighting the same battles, one shelter and pound at a time. We're initiating viable programs to combat the tired mentality of shelter and pound directors who continue to embrace killing as a method of population control.

We've helped transform high-kill shelters into No Kill facilities, one at a time. In our own county, we've worked relentlessly for more than 11 years to try and work with our own county pound (which saves a mere 18% of healthy, friendly cats who enter their doors each year). After more than a decade of persistence, we're now the first approved rescue to be given permission to pull death row cats from this facility. But we still have a long way to go. After more than a decade of operating Advocates 4 Animals, we have established a handful of robust programs to combat our local pound's tired and outdated policies. Collaboration is generally the best route for helping the animals, but when you have a slaughter house (aka high-kill county pound) that refuses to embrace *any* life-saving measures, you do your best to keep animals out of their "care" by any and all means. Over the years, in addition to our rescue/rehabilitation/adoption program, we have established a pet food pantry to provide temporary pet food assistance to families facing financial hardship. By providing pet food, families are able to keep their pets with them, rather than relinquish them to the pound and a terrible fate. We have established an affordable spay/neuter program for cats within our own county, again to help humanely control the pet population and to keep pets from being turned in to the pound. We have a Community Cats program which works to train and assist the public in TNR (trap-neuter-release) for feral cats. These, among other programs are helping us lower the rate of animals entering the local pound; therefore decreasing the number of needless deaths perpetuated by that very pound.

Across the country, additional animal rescue/adoption, spay/neuter program and pet food pantry programs are urgently needed. One of the most popular questions we are asked is "How can I start a rescue?" It's not a simple one-word answer. If you do it right, you are actively helping animals in need. It may look "easy" to those on the outside, but as with anything worth doing, the endeavor of creating a non-profit (i.e. for purpose) animal welfare organization is filled with endless hard work, dedication, compassion, and perhaps most importantly a strong business sense. Yes, operating an animal rescue or animal welfare organization is a business. If you're considering starting an animal rescue organization you must have a plan in place and you must operate as a business.

The chapters ahead outline the basics of what you'll need to consider prior to starting an organization of your own. While the need for helping animals is ever present, the need for creating a viable, sustainable organization is essential. Don't fret: if you do not want to start your own organization and you're simply interested in understanding more about animal rescue this book is for you too! Whether you wish to help one or two animals a year through fostering for an organization, or you hope to start your own organization, this book is for you. The chapters ahead share the fundamental elements necessary to start an animal welfare organization *the right way.* In addition, we share our own experiences with you along the way. From hilarious mishaps to tough lessons, we share some of our most memorable stories throughout the book in hopes of helping you find your own path toward helping animals in need. Although everyone's journey will be unique, we can promise you one thing; if you devote even a portion of your life to helping animals in need, you will, at times be blissfully covered in pet fur.

SPECIAL NOTE: Many chapters in this book are followed by a "challenge" page which consists of both thought-provoking and action seeking questions to consider in regard to your own community and the animals you wish to help.

CHAPTER 1: PAWS & CONSIDER THE FACTS...

WHILE WAITING ON A FOSTER HOME SPACE to become available, we asked the Good Samaritans who contacted us at Advocates 4 Animals to help a mom cat and her newborn babies, if they could safely keep her inside of their home until we had an opening two days later. They agreed and we were happy to have space to help. We work to save death row shelter pets on a daily basis and we work to combat cats ever entering the shelter through our rescue/adoption program. All of our foster/adoptable pets are housed in individual volunteer foster homes and the number of lives we can save is always dependent on the number of quality, trained foster homes we have in our network. The constant pressure to help is enormous as it comes from pet guardians wanting to surrender their pets for one reason or another, from strays found in the public, from abuse and neglect cases, from feral cat colonies and from local kill shelters. Add to that, in 2013 our local pound only saved a mere 18% of "healthy, adoptable" cats and kittens. The pressure that we face on a day-to-day basis is life versus death. If we don't step up to help, there are no "back-up's" to call on in our area.

But I digress...two days later we were elated to help a mom cat and her newborn kittens and we traveled to the address given to rescue them. We knocked on the door to the house several times prior to receiving an answer. The door creaked open as a large dog lunged toward us. The man was confused and the home was dark. I waited outside by the car, ready with food and water. Amy walked into the house letting the door close behind her as the dog stayed close at her heels watching her every move. The man retreated to an even darker basement and a moment later appeared with a sealed Tupperware container which he handed over. The mom and her newborn kittens were inside. Amy scurried out of the house as quickly as she could and as she approached the car, she threw open the lid to the box and we found that only one kitten remained alive. The box was full of steam as the mom cat had urinated and defecated while sealed in the box for two days. They all sat in the dampness of her excrement. The one newborn baby who had survived was barely hanging on. His eyes were not open yet and he was gasping for air; it had been too long. Meanwhile, the mom cat took in her first few breaths of fresh air in days. She was covered in the wetness of her own waste, terribly emaciated and dangerously dehydrated. We poured a fresh bowl of water and watched her lap up the smooth liquid with enthusiasm. Next we opened a can of wet cat food and she devoured the food with vigor. Afterwards she moved towards her only surviving kitten to bathe him and curled up in a ball amongst the nest of blankets we had created for her in her large pet crate. The gray and white mom cat couldn't have been more than a year old herself. We named her Libby and sadly her remaining baby did not survive the night. Libby was exhausted and defeated, although we knew she appreciated the constant love, affection, fresh food, water and veterinary care; her heart was broken.

After nearly two months of physical and emotional rehabilitation in her foster home, we were working on a project to save three death row shelter kittens. Libby's foster mom agreed to foster the kittens, along with Libby. Magically within moments of being introduced to each other, Libby began to mother the three orphaned kittens (new fosters). She bathed them, cuddled with them and watched over them and as she did this, her own broken heart began to heal.

The need for the rescue of companion animals is astounding. United States shelters currently kill more than 50% of adoptable cats and dogs annually; a number that can be drastically changed for the better as additional qualified rescue organizations are established and as competent, compassionate shelter directors are hired. In our own county, less than 18% of healthy, adoptable cats left the pound alive in 2013; while a mere 30% of healthy, adoptable dogs left the shelter doors alive. The rest left in body bags, as if they never existed or mattered. Those innocent pets who are left in body bags were owner surrendered pets (guardians who said they were moving, didn't have enough time for the pet, had a baby, had sudden allergies, et cetera), they were feral cats who could have lived out their lives on one of the many local farms after being altered, they were neglected and abused pets who hid in the back of their cramped cages afraid someone new might harm them. They were senior pets who the shelter saw as "unadoptable" and unwanted. They were special needs pets who may have looked a bit different but could have lived long, happy, healthy lives nonetheless. They were black cats and dogs who because of the color of their fur are quickly deemed "unadoptable" as they are so often not the first picks among adopters. They were living, breathing lives who just wanted a chance to survive, but due to one shelter director's daily decisions, they didn't get that chance. Their fate had been decided for them by those who turned them into the shelter; the decision to kill them being finalized by the shelter director.

We've worked with countless open intake shelters as they begin their journeys to become No Kill communities. It is possible to work together when a collaborative effort is established. In our own county, we worked for 11 years until we were finally given clearance to be the first approved rescue organization to work with the pound to pull *some* of the death row pets in need. It's a start, but a great deal more is needed. While in the shelter recently to save a batch of orphaned kittens, a terrified young mom cat and her two-week old kittens sat in one of the nearby cages. Our volunteer asked if we could pull them too. She explained that she had room to foster a new feline family in need now. The director said the mom cat was "feral" (although she appeared to simply be scared in the cramped, loud environment of the shelter). Our foster volunteer said that she didn't mind if the mom cat was scared and she was willing to work with her on socialization. In addition, she offered that if the mom did turn out to be feral, she lived on several acres of land and had heated cat huts and would allow the altered cat to live freely on her property once the babies were weaned. The shelter director shot her down instantly, fighting for what he saw as control and telling her "I'm not comfortable with that." Instead of letting the cat live, instead of letting the cat go to a foster home and eventually a forever home, he saw the death of a nursing mom cat as a better solution. A week later, we received a call that the two orphaned kittens needed rescue and to be bottle-fed. Their mom was no longer here to do the feeding (the shelter had killed her). So although we have made great strides in being "approved" to pull from the local pound, there is a lot more work to be done.

Pets in need are all ages, breeds and sizes. One day while at the shelter to save several cats in need, we came across two large adult cats huddled together in their small cage. We were told the cats were owner surrendered and no veterinary paperwork or records had been left, they hadn't even passed along their names. So there they sat, huddled together, holding each other in their dark cage, not knowing what would happen next. But we knew they were next in line to leave in a body bag that day. After making a few calls to our foster homes we were able to secure a foster home for the two of them together in our network and we successfully pulled the two adult cats to safety. They had been previously spayed/neutered and declawed and on the ride home they continued to hold each other, the female wrapping her arms around the back of the male.

Rescue is needed when it's done the right way. Over more than a decade of working in animal rescue, we've encountered both rescues and shelters who operate on the fly. That's when things quickly go south for the animals in need. All too often, those who start a rescue organization have big hearts but a lack of business sense. They want to save the animals, their intentions are positive, but the follow through is lacking. When you agree to take in an animal as a foster pet in your rescue, the animals must receive proper testing and veterinary care prior to entering the foster homes (more on this later). It is also important to verify that the foster homes' personal pets are up to date on vaccinations, healthy and spayed/neutered. Furthermore, the foster home needs to be the right match for the new foster pet. If you have a terribly shy or frightened pet and you place him in a lively foster home with children and other pets, issues are going to arise quickly. Operating an animal rescue isn't just about saving the animals, it's about providing proper veterinary care for every pet (first and foremost spay/neuter), proper food, water, shelter and adequate love, attention and rehabilitation training. In addition, how will you find qualified adopters for each of your pets? What will you do if you have an aggressive pet? Rescuing the pet is just the tip of the iceberg. What follows requires a strong business model, hard work and one of the most important aspects of running any business…great communication skills!

When individuals contact you for assistance, you should reply within 48 hours of their request and should always offer guidance. Operating an animal rescue organization is a 24/7 business; you don't get a break on holidays or birthdays. You will not be able to take in every pet that you are asked to help, but you can always offer other resources that may be able to provide a solution to help the animal in need. **Your words have the power to help, as much as your actions.**

When my own dog passed away from old age, I was devastated. Her name was Grandma and we rescued her from a shelter after she was deemed vicious and unadoptable. She was a senior dog at the time and in horrible health. She was a foster pet turned forever pet for me. She fit in great with my other two rescue dogs and we had three wonderful years together before she passed. At Advocates 4 Animals, our rescue focus is on cats. After a bit of time, I felt ready to save another senior dog in need and I began my search. I contacted shelters, pounds and rescue organizations alike in search of a senior dog who needed help. I wanted to provide a senior dog with a loving home, who would otherwise not have one. But my search only lead to endless frustration and for the first time I found myself on the opposite side of the adoption table. Instead of being the foster mom who helped potential adopters find the right match, I was now the potential adopter in search of assistance myself. Or rather, I should say I was in search of a reply! We contacted close to twenty area rescues, shelters and pounds and in the first week we only were able to actually speak with two. One was a kill shelter in Indiana who had four potential senior dogs needing help, but the individual we spoke with didn't know anything about them. The other was a dog focused rescue organization who was pleasantly responsive and helpful. As for the other 18 organizations, we were left without a reply. We called, left countless messages, wrote emails introducing ourselves and even filled out adoption applications…all were left without a reply. More than a month after the inquiries (and after we had found and adopted a special needs senior dog from the local dog rescue organization who had kindly responded the same week we contacted them) we received two more replies that were short and unhelpful. One said they wanted to know which dog we were interested in (even though it clearly stated the dog's name in our original email they were replying to) the other reply said that they would work on getting back to us. We never heard back from any of the others. It was a real wake-up call for what adopters are experiencing! It wasn't just from pounds or shelters, it was from rescue organizations too. The lack of response was disheartening. Our focus from the beginning at Advocates 4 Animals has always been on responsiveness and communication (and it is difficult when you are bombarded with hundreds of emails, texts and phone calls on a daily basis) but it is do-able if you make communication one of your priorities. It is a must for any successful business model. Without communication, you cannot find foster homes, adopters, donors, et cetera for your operation. Friendly, respectful and responsive communication is essential. Set specific hours during the work week and weekends which you will devote to e-mails, phone calls and other forms of communication and stick to it. As with any viable business, you will ride the roller-coaster of ups and downs. Be sure to realize that your top concerns are the welfare of the animals in your care and your daily communications with potential adopters, your foster homes, volunteers and potential donors.

At Advocates 4 Animals, it's always our goal to provide each potential adopter with a positive experience so that in the future, if they decide to add to their furry family, they will choose to adopt a rescue pet again. Whether it's from us or another rescue or shelter organization, our goal is to promote the adoption of rescue pets and to help each adopter have a memorable experience that they will then share with others. With some eight million rescue pets waiting for homes annually in our country alone, we need to do everything we can to promote adoption into loving, committed homes.

CHAPTER 1- CHALLENGE:

- What are the euthanasia statistics at your local pound and/or shelter? What are their intake numbers and where are the majority of their intakes coming from (i.e. owner surrenders, senior pets, ill pets, etc.?) Is the shelter/pound an open-intake facility? Is their director willing to work with local 501(c)3 rescue organizations?

- How many 501(c)3 rescue organizations are in your area? Are they volunteer-based? Do they have facilities? What is each rescue organizations main focus (i.e. dogs under 10-pounds, a specific breed of dog, et cetera)?

- How many 501(c)3 organizations work to help feral cats in your area (through TNR methods)?

DON'T DELAY...
PURCHASE TODAY!
Available on Amazon in paperback and e-book formats